Roscoe Conkling

The Constitution and presidential Elections

Roscoe Conkling

The Constitution and presidential Elections

ISBN/EAN: 9783743324787

Manufactured in Europe, USA, Canada, Australia, Japa

Cover: Foto ©ninafisch / pixelio.de

Manufactured and distributed by brebook publishing software
(www.brebook.com)

Roscoe Conkling

The Constitution and presidential Elections

SPEECH

OF

ROSCOE CONKLING,

IN THE

SENATE OF THE UNITED STATES,

JANUARY 23 AND 24, 1877.

"Justice, is law executed."

WASHINGTON.
1877.

SPEECH

OF

ROSCOE CONKLING.

The Senate having under consideration the bill (S. No. 1153) to provide for and regulate the counting of the votes for President and Vice-President, and the decision of questions arising thereon, for the term commencing March 4, A. D. 1877—

Mr. CONKLING said:

Mr. PRESIDENT: Before reaching the details of this measure or its advantages or wisdom, we must make sure of the power, in some mode, to subject the verification and count of electoral votes to the action of the two Houses, or to the law-making power. A study of the question years ago, convinced me of the right and therefore the duty of the two Houses, to ascertain and verify electoral votes and declare the true result of presidential elections, or else by an exertion of the law-making power to declare how these acts shall be done. My present judgment does not rest however wholly on preconceived opinions. Some weeks ago, when the inquiry came to be invested with unprecedented importance, I reviewed carefully every act and proceeding in our history bearing upon it, and, without the aid then of compilations made since, every utterance in regard to it to be found in books.

A distinction may be drawn between the power of the Senate and the House themselves to execute this duty directly by force of the Constitution alone, and the power of Congress by law to direct it to be done in any way other than strictly and literally by the two Houses. It is not my purpose at this moment to explore this distinction, nor to inquire how far, or whether at all, the Constitution inculcates the exact mode or form in which the two Houses, or Congress, shall execute the twelfth article. If the function and duty there commanded be within the province of the two Houses, or if the Constitution leaves to the law-making power the right to declare the mode by which presidential elections shall be verified, the proposed bill is competent, as I may attempt hereafter to show. If the two Houses are themselves by the Constitution commanded to count the votes, the bill executes the Constitution. If, however, the true meaning of article 12 merely commands the votes to be counted, without declaring by whom they shall be counted, then Congress, the repository of "all legislative powers," is directed how to proceed by the concluding words of section 8, article 1. It is there ordained that—

The Congress shall have power to make all laws which shall be necessary and proper for carrying into execution the foregoing powers, and all other powers vested by this Constitution in the Government of the United States, or in any department or officer thereof.

But if the power in question is deposited by the Constitution, and is not deposited with the two Houses, neither the bill on the table nor any bill, rule, or plan seeking to draw the count of electoral votes, or their examination, within the jurisdiction of the two Houses or of Congress, is of the slightest efficacy or validity. If, by the Constitution, the Senate and House are only spectators of the count, there is an end of the matter as to them and as to each of them. Any action by either House, is then sheer intrusion—any statute proposing action, is null, and an attempt to violate the Constitution by usurping powers it withholds. If the power to ascertain and count is vested in the President of the Senate, perhaps the form of his proceeding—for example whether he shall take up the States alphabetically or otherwise in opening certificates, might be prescribed by law. But any act or rule to strip him of the power or of any part of the power reposed in him by the Constitution, would be plainly void. The Constitution declares that the President of the United States shall be Commander-in-Chief of the Army and Navy. A statute declaring the Secretary of State, or any body save only the President alone, Commander-in-Chief, or putting any one in partnership with him as Commander-in-Chief, would be null. Nor does it alter the case if the Constitution vests power by implication rather than by express words. It matters not what words are employed, whether they be palpably explicit, or so general or few that resort must be had to construction to ascertain their force and meaning. Whenever a power is by the Constitution, in any form of words whatever, deposited with an officer or department, there it is, and there it must remain as long as the Constitution remains unaltered.

It has never been seriously contended, at least never until of late, it never was seriously contended until we had "a case on hand," if I may borrow a phrase from a distinguished Senator, that this power belongs to one House alone, or to one House more than to the other. Most of those who challenge the competency of a bill dealing with the subject, maintain that the power resides in the President of the Senate. If then the bill before the Senate executes the Constitution whether the twelfth article requires the count to be by the two Houses literally, or only requires that Congress shall cause it to be made, it cannot trench on the Constitution unless the President of the Senate is endowed with the power to conduct and determine the count.

This question I propose to examine by the text of the Constitution, aided by the settled rules of construction, by the opinions of the most illustrious men of four generations, and by the practice and acquiescence of the nation and of all departments of the Government for eighty-seven years.

The President of the Senate is clearly the person to whom the electors are to transmit, in a sealed packet, the certificate of their own appointment, and of the ballots they cast—he is clearly the person who is to keep these packets, and keep them inviolate, till the day comes when the law says that Congress shall be in session, the certificates shall be opened, the votes counted, "and the persons who shall fill the offices of President and Vice-President ascertained and declared agreeably to the Constitution."

How the President of the Senate, rather than some other person or officer, came to be selected as the custodian of these sealed packets, we are not left to conjecture. The history of the formation of the Constitution informs us. The selection was made in a draught or plan afterwards disapproved in its chief feature. By that plan it was proposed to give to the Senate alone the choice of the President in case of a failure by the electors to choose him. An incident, and a natural incident of this arrangement, was to commit the custody of the certificates to the presiding officer of the body which was to elect the President if none was found to have been chosen. This proposal was rejected, and the power to choose the President in case none had been chosen by the electors of the States, was conferred on the House of Representatives. Other changes were made, but the original draught served throughout as the basis of action. Alterations were made in it, but without discarding it totally and beginning anew, just as alterations are usually made in a bill by amendments, one at a time, instead of rejecting the whole bill in gross, and substituting a new one for it.

One of the details not thus altered, was the designation of him who should receive and keep, and be responsible for till they were needed, and then produce, the electoral certificates.

With or without this ray of light falling on the few words whose meaning we must learn, one thing will probably be admitted by all. It will not be denied that had any other officer been denoted as the President of the Senate is, his duty, power, and prerogative, would be exactly the same. Had the President of the United States, or the Secretary of State, or the Speaker of the House, or the Secretary of the Senate, or the Clerk of the House, been the officer named, in either case the same words would confer on him the same power and impose the same duty now reposed in the President of the Senate—neither more or less.

This brings me to the language of Article Twelve of the Constitution.

It is there declared that the electors shall meet in their respective States, and, within certain restrictions, vote for President and Vice-President, and that they shall make and certify a statement of their proceedings and transmit it sealed to the seat of Government directed to the President of the Senate. The contents were to be a secret. The purpose was to commit to the unpledged discretion of the electors, they being relied on as a body of sagacious unbiased men, the absolute selection of a Chief Magistrate choosing from the whole body of the people. In aid of this purpose they were required to vote by ballot so that even bystanders might not know how an elector voted, or for whom votes were given. To secure and continue secrecy, the votes were to be enveloped under seal, that curiosity might not pry into them, or fraud, alter or destroy them, till they were disclosed to the whole nation. A responsible and trustworthy custodian was essential to their inviolate preservation. The modern practice of parties has overturned the idea of unpledged electors, and now electors represent particular candidates nominated in advance; the Constitution however remains, and knowing its purpose, the confidence reposed in this regard in the President of the Senate would not be belittling to the highest functionary on earth. An act of 1792, re-enacted in 1874 as part of the Revised Statutes, amplifies and defines the duties of the electors, and among other things requires them to annex to the certificates of their proceedings the evidence of their own appointments.

Pursuing the Constitution, we find these words following those already referred to:

The President of the Senate shall, in the presence of the Senate and House of Representatives, open all the certificates, and the votes shall then be counted.

A familiar maxim of construction is, that meaning and effect must be given, as far as may be, to every word. This is true of the most trifling agreement between men. It must be at least as true of a frame of government laboriously devised and meant to stand as an eternal wedlock between peoples and states. The first words we meet here are "in the presence of the Senate and House of Representatives." The consequence attached to these words may **be** somewhat **inferred** from occurrences in the First and Second Congresses, in which **sat eighteen** of the thirty-nine men who framed the Constitution. **By an act of** Congress they required that on the day when the persons **shall be** ascertained and declared who shall fill the offices of **President** and Vice-President "the Congress shall be in session." **Perhaps the first question** which arises is for what was the Congress **thus twice required to be** in session? Obviously for some act, or, that **its members may be** spectators—they could hardly be witnesses of **such an act in** any reasonable sense if the act is to be done exclusively **by one person.** If the President of the Senate alone, is empowered to **determine what** shall be counted, and to count, and adjudge the re-**sult, it is not easy to see how** the two Houses can in any just and **ef-fectual sense witness and verify** the truth of that he does. They can **hear what the officer says if he** chooses to say anything, but nothing **requires** him to speak a word. No declaration even at the end, is re-quired by **the** Constitution. The whole proceeding may be in silence. But if the custodian of the certificates, after they are opened, chooses **to** state **their contents or** effect, and this he all, the whole transaction **is** his. **He takes up a paper** in his **seat** and peruses it as he would pe-**ruse a letter. The Senators** and Representatives see him from the body **of the Hall, but they no more see or** know the signatures or seals or **words or figures appearing on the** paper, than if they gazed at the **spectacle from the galleries,** or saw it as a concourse **sees** the oath of **office administered to the** President on the eastern portico of the **Capitol. If the President** of the Senate announces that **no one has a majority, the House must** either accept the statement, **though it may be believed erroneous, and** proceed to an election, or **the House must disregard the statement** and **refuse to** proceed. The Constitu-**tion plainly states the hinge** whereon **the** action of the House must **turn. Saying nothing about what any one** shall say **or declare,** arti-**cle 12, dealing with the fundamental fact,** ordains that **if no one has in truth received a majority of all the** votes, and of all **the electors** appointed, the **House of Representatives** shall immediately **choose** the President. **The fact proved by the** votes, is made the **sole crite-**rion, and whether **it was intended that the** House should **act** on what the President of the Senate might say about th**e fact, or on** what the House itself might know or believe about the **fact,** is an inquiry I commend to those who suppose that only **one** person, and he not con-nected with the House, is authorized to examine the votes and deter-mine their validity and effect. If the members of either House sus-pected forgery or error, **as** matter of right they could take no proceed-ing relating to the count, **and** if the act of the President of the Senate is effectual and binding, it would afterward be too **late. It must,** however, be admitted **not**withstanding all this, that these words **in and of** themselves **may be** satisfied by supposing that the two **Houses,** consisting now **of about four** hundred members, are **required to be** present with their **officers** merely to behold a pageant, **to** see **and be seen, as spectators of an occasion** wherein they **can** act no part.

The text proceeds. The President **of** the Senate shall "open all the certificates." There **is no** room for construction here. This is a plain grant of power to do **a** certain simple thing and a direction to do it. Now the language changes. "The President of the Senate" is drop-ped; he disappears, and nowhere re-appears: "And the votes shall then be counted." That is, a count of the votes shall then take place: a **count** of the votes shall then be had. "The votes shall then be counted." By whom? By him? As two Senators have inquired, why was it not said "by him?" How easy to add these two little words, "by him!" The men who drafted this solemn instrument, masters of language as most of them were, were so fastidious in taste, so scrupulous in the execution of their work, so determined that words should become exact vehicles of thought, that they appointed a committee on style in order that every syllable might do its needed office. How, Mr. President, would men only ordinarily instructed in the English language have expressed themselves had they intended that the President of the Senate should count the votes? "The President of the Senate shall, in the presence of the Senate and House of Representatives, open all the certificates and count the votes," are the words which ninety and nine men in a hundred would naturally have written or spoken. Had they said "the President of the Senate shall count the votes" simply, that would have been plain. Why? Because no man can count or examine the contents of a sealed packet without opening it, and there implication would have made all plain. So had they said "open and count the votes." But no, he "shall open all the certificates, and the votes shall *then* be counted." Why "then?" If the President of the Senate was to open and count, if it was to be one act at one time in one place by one person, all parts of the act must of necessity be "then," must they not? Why bring in the word "then?" But why change the current of the sentence, and why use twice as many words as were necessary or natural, when the effect of doing so would be to bewilder, if not mislead, the reader? The Constitution is terse, sententious, a model of comprehensive brevity. You scan it in vain for another instance of a phrase so loose and needlessly wordy, if indeed the intent was to say that the person who was to open the certificates should also count.

In the first instance these words "in the presence of the Senate and House of Representatives" were proposed not before the word "counted" but after the word "counted;" so that it would have stood and it did stand "the votes shall then be counted in the presence of the Senate and House of Representatives." In the earlier considerations of the convention the words so standing were accepted more than once. At length the provision was referred to the committee on style, and I beg to inquire for what purpose? To change the meaning of those who by little accretions of concurrence had built up step by step with patience and care a great fabric of government, destined as they believed to stand so strong and last so long? Was the purpose of the committee on style and of those who trusted the committee, to take liberties with substance, and to change the essence as it had been agreed to? O, no, but to define the meaning more sharply, to project it more distinctly and unmistakbly before the minds of those who in a far future would appeal to this instrument as the testament and revelation of free institutions. When the committee reported these words to the consideration of the convention for final and perfected action, they stood as they stand now "in the presence of the Senate and House of Representatives, open all the certificates, and the votes shall then be counted." Was it ever, in all the scrutiny which those words underwent, proposed to use such words as would commit the power compressed into the word "count," to the President of the Senate? Were any of the forms I have suggested or other forms clearly denoting that, ever proposed at all? No, sir; but on the contrary, after all this care, and painstaking, the words as we see them were adopted, as the last, most deliberate, consummate act of the constitutional convention.

If we thoughtfully read these words, and the change they introduce into the sentence, several intents appear in dropping the President of the Senate and employing the present phrase "the votes shall then be counted." What "votes?" Not all votes. "All the certificates" are to be opened, but not all votes are to be counted. "The votes" are to "be counted." What votes? The constitutional, valid, true votes; not six votes from Oregon although six appear; not necessarily the three votes certified by the governor of Oregon although he is the certifying officer by the act of 1792 and the only certifying officer known to the national laws; but the three honest votes, if there are three. These three, and only these, are to be counted. Counting and ascertaining becomes substantial, and we see reasons for so making it, if we recur only to the exclusions provided by the Constitution. The honorable Senator from Indiana said yesterday that the President of the Senate—I borrow his phrase—is to count everything "good, bad, and indifferent." Mr. President I dissent from this position. The act of 1792 already referred to declares, speaking of the proceedings in question:

> That Congress shall be in session * * * and the said certificates, or so many of them as shall have been received, shall then be opened, the votes counted, and *the persons who shall fill the offices of President and Vice-President ascertained and declared, agreeably to the Constitution.*

The Constitution names five instances in which no majority of votes shall work the ascertainment to fill the office of President of the United States. Was it designed that votes cast for one dead should be counted, and that he should fill with an aching void the office of President of the United States? Would that be "agreeable" to the Constitution? Was it designed that votes forged should be counted; votes, not certified or certified by an usurper, counted blindly and without inquiry? Was it designed, if lying on our table be a record denouncing against a convict on impeachment perpetual exclusion from every office of profit, emolument, or trust, that votes cast for him should be counted and made effectual, and this, because although not good, such votes might be "bad or indifferent?" No, Mr. President. Should the State of Massachusetts send here an electoral certificate on which should appear as the first two electors the names of my honored friends the Senators from Massachusetts, and if then should follow as electors the name of every Representative from Massachusetts, designating them respectively as Senators and Representatives, I should read in the Constitution that "no Senator or Representative" shall be or shall even be "appointed an elector," and I should say those votes, although they might be "bad" or "indifferent," were not to be held good until they were at least considered. "Agreeably to the Constitution" some heed must be given to its plain and absolute prohibitions, and "bad" votes, that is to say forbidden votes, are not of course or by main force to be counted as if they were "good" votes, which is to say legal and constitutional votes.

But, it has been said that the power of the President of the Senate, though not expressed in the Constitution, may be implied from that which is expressed. It has been whispered that the President of the Senate may, in a closet or a corner, a month in advance, adjudge, determine, and conclude the electoral count by refusing to receive any certificate except that which he chooses in the end to count. That is, he may decide that he will receive two certificates from Oregon, that being a large if not a populous State, but that one each must suffice for all the other States, and so he would take but one. The existing President of the Senate, discharging as he habitually does, with conscience and propriety, the duties resting on him, has already, I am informed, received contesting certificates from the three or four States from which they come. I have heard no one say aloud that having received them, it will be his duty or prerogative to suppress or conceal any of them; and therefore I proceed to consider whether by implication he has the power to judge between them, to determine what shall become of them, and what is their legal import and quality.

The doctrine of implication stretched to cover the ground here involved, may be said to derive implication from implication, or rather to craft implication on implication. The argument seems to be first, that because the President of the Senate is the custodian of the certificates and directed to open them, it may be implied that he has power afterward to count the votes they contain; and then from that implied power it may be implied that he has the power to determine what shall be counted: and then from this second implied power may be implied the power to decide and affirm the effect of the count he has made, and of the votes he has held valid.

The argument in favor of the authority of the President of the Senate certainly deserves respectful consideration. It has found no voice in this debate. It is a position against which, if I mistake not, every member of this body on both sides, save four, stands on his oath recorded. I repeat it has found no voice in this debate; but I receive it respectfully as a suggestion which I must weigh carefully, because beyond these walls the thought has been advanced by those whose words and opinions are entitled to be weighed.

The doctrine of implication or implied powers as long and unchangably known to the law, may thus be stated: When power is given to do a thing, permission is implied to employ the means to do it. Whatever is essential to the full and complete execution or enjoyment of a thing granted, is deemed to be granted also. Experience abounds in illustration of this species of intendment. A spot of ground is granted in the midst of a great field. It is implied that the grantee has granted to him also a right to pass over the intervening ground to get to his possession. When the Constitution empowers Congress to coin money, to borrow money, to establish post-offices and post-roads, power is implied to resort to the needed ways and means, and thus, to authorize banks, and mints, the acquirement of real estate, and the like. This is the doctrine of the old Supreme Court with Marshall at its head, in McCulloch vs. Maryland, in Weston vs. The City of Charleston; and in many noted cases since. When the Constitution authorizes the President on the call of a governor or Legislature to employ troops upon the happening of a certain contingency, the power is implied in him to inquire and determine whether that contingency has arisen. So said the Supreme Court in the case of Mott vs. Martin. But the terminus and boundaries of this doctrine, are as certain as legal bounds can be. Whatever is essential or conveniently conducive to, or fairly in aid of a granted power, may be implied or inferred; but nothing more. Here is the end, in reason, and in law.

Implication operates in favor of the right to do an act minor to and involved in something beyond which is expressly authorized. Power to do a limited and defined thing, does not ordinarily work power to do a greater thing—the greater contains the less, not the less the greater. Power to do an act of one species or nature, does not work by implication power to do a separate act of a different species or nature, particularly an act of more exalted nature, not essential to the act expressly authorized. Power to do a ministerial act does not imply power to act judicially. Authority to act as custodian of papers, does not confer license to exercise transcendent powers of sovereignty, or of supreme ultimate political and public determination. Express authority to do a given thing never implies power to do anything whatever after the act authorized is completely done and ended. The certificates must be opened before their contents can be examined or passed upon—they must be opened before counting their contents can begin: how then can power to judge and ascertain afterward, be inferred from power to produce and open beforehand? How can the latter be incident to the former? Breaking the seals is merely prefatory to a wholly different proceeding.

A clerk of a court, or the presiding justice, is made the recipient and custodian of papers—he is to keep them untouched and sealed till a certain day, and then he is to carry them into court and open them. Would a statute declaring that the papers should then be acted on, or should then undergo examination, or that facts of which they were evidential should then be found, mean that the clerk, or the one justice, and not the court, was to act on the papers, or pass upon them, or find the facts from them, and would his power to do any or all of these things be implied from the fact of his being the custodian of the packet?

If, in the instance supposed, the sheriff were the custodian, and the contents of the packet were warrants and summons, and the statute declared that these writs should then be served, how should we know who was to serve them? The appropriateness of the sheriff for such a purpose would suggest him as the proper person, but this is not all. We should know it was the sheriff who should act, because the law declares that the sheriff shall serve all such writs.

But in the case supposed if the statute said "and the validity and effect of the writs shall then be passed upon," should we infer that the sheriff was to pass upon them, and this because the law made him their custodian? We should know the court was to do this, merely because the function is judicial and the court is a judicial body and so authorized by law.

Apply the rule to the matter before us. We know too well the nature of the possible inquiries involved. Committees have gone far and wide to conduct them. My distinguished friend from Wisconsin [Mr. HOWE] has pained us by his absence for weeks, because deputed by the Senate to tarry in a distant State. Many other Senators have done the like. The framers of the Constitution knew and pondered the sort of problems which might arise for solution; they have left us evidence that they were not unmindful of some of the questions which now confront us.

My inquiry at this point is whether the President of the Senate is so equipped for settling disputed questions of fact, is so endowed with facilities for resolving problems like these, that reason and intendment point to him alone as the tribunal to decide?

The person having the largest number of votes, of valid, legal votes, be it a majority, is to be the President. The question is, who "shall fill the office of President?" The Constitution has named, as I said, at least five cases in which, although a majority of votes be given for a candidate, he shall not fill the office of President. No person shall fill the office of President unless he be a native-born citizen; no person shall fill the office of President unless he has attained the age of five and thirty years; no person shall fill the office of President unless he has been fourteen years a resident of the country; no person shall fill the office of President chosen by the votes of electors in the State wherein he resides who voted also for another person in the same State for Vice-President; no person shall fill the office of President who, having been impeached by the grand inquest of the nation, has been branded by the votes of two-thirds of this body and immutably disqualified. The certificates may be forgeries, the pretended electors may not be the true electors, he who assumes as governor to certify the electors may not be the governor at all. These and other questions may arise; still higher and larger questions may arise. Has the President of the Senate power to send for persons and papers; to compel the surrender of telegrams, and imprison witnesses if they will not give them up? Who has that power? Who had it when the Constitution was made? Was there any body who familiarly in both hemispheres had wielded such power? Yes, sir, the British Parliament for ages had possessed and exercised the power to judge of the election, qualifications, and returns of officials. The State Legislatures on this continent had done the same thing. Joint meetings of two legislative houses had long been common. It had been customary for the Lords and Commons to assemble in joint conference, and their rules relative to such meetings, more than two centuries old, stand I believe even to this day. So, after our Constitution was adopted it was customary for the Senate and House to meet and sit together to receive the message or speech of the President of the United States. The two houses of State Legislatures, from the beginning, have assembled together; they do so still, not only to elect regents of universities, not only to choose Senators in Congress, but to see opened, to canvass, to ascertain, to determine the count of votes and the results of elections. The honorable Senator from Ohio sits before me [Mr. THURMAN] and seeing him reminds me of an ancient custom in his State. As early perhaps as 1802 the State of Ohio had I think in its fundamental law substantially the words of our Constitution "the presiding officer shall open the certificates in the presence of the two houses and the votes shall then be counted." Was this the provision?

Mr. THURMAN. Pretty nearly.

Mr. CONKLING. I ask the Senator from Ohio to correct me if I am wrong in saying that even at that early day and always during the maintenance of that constitution, it was the settled and uncontested understanding that the presiding officer merely opened the certificates, and that the two houses of the Legislature of Ohio together proceeded to count or canvass the votes. Am I right in that?

Mr. THURMAN. That is right as to the governor.

Mr. EDMUNDS. The chief magistrate.

Mr. CONKLING. The chief magistrate of the State. I ask then whether it can be doubted that the men who employed the words "and the votes shall then be counted" knew of a tribunal or body having powers and faculties adequate to the conduct of such a proceeding?

It has been said that the count is a mere addition of units; that nothing is needed to count except common honesty and common sense. I do not understand the word to be so employed in the Constitution. Counting may be of different kinds. To count my fingers is a purely ministerial act and very simple. To count a pile of papers is a ministerial act. To count bank-notes in which there may be counterfeits; and separate the true from the false, is more than a ministerial act, it requires judgment; it involves faculty. To "open all the certificates" is a ministerial act; as my honorable friend from Vermont [Mr. EDMUNDS] suggests, as a porter might open a bale of goods. It is purely a ministerial act. But to count the votes, is something more.

Why? "All the certificates" are to be opened; **but** not all votes are **to be** counted. The valid, constitutional votes, **and no** other votes, are **to** counted; and he who counts them, with his **fan in** his hand, must winnow the wheat from the chaff, if there be chaff. If New York sends 45 votes as electoral votes, they are not all to be counted, because New York is entitled to only 35 electoral votes. They are to be sorted, the bad and indifferent are to be separated from the good, and only the 35 true constitutional votes are to be counted; because they who were intruders or ignorantly added their names to the roll, did **an** act unauthorized, and therefore void. If the certificate of Massachusetts should by accident or fraud show that her votes were cast for the democratic candidates, the world knows that Massachusetts voted for the republican nominees, and, therefore, the certificate is **not to** be blindly counted, or counted at all without inquiry and **verification.** If electoral votes are cast **for Julius** Cæsar—or for Harry the **Eighth, or a** British subject—they **are not to be** counted without inquiry.

An illustration of the difference between these two kinds **of counting, may be found in an** incident of the last examination **of electoral votes. In** 1873, **four electors** of the State of Georgia voted **for Horace Greeley. What was the objection to** that? Why should they not vote **for one of the most eminent members** of one of the largest professions? **What was the difficulty? Was there** any doubt that the electors **were appointed? No, sir. Was there** objection to their election? **No, sir. Was not Georgia a State in the** Union? Had not every propriety **and mandate been observed? Yes,** sir. But a Representative **from the State of Massachusetts rose in the** meeting of the two Houses **and said:**

I object to the count of those votes; I object because it is announced that Mr. Greeley was buried on the day on which those votes were cast.

Let me be more explicit with the Senate in stating the process of **the member who made the objection. Legally** dissected, his statement **was this:** "The certificate is blameless on its face; **there** is a State behind it; these four men were legal electors; but the newspapers have announced that Mr. Greeley was buried on the day the votes were cast; nobody has said he was buried alive, therefore it may be concluded, and the Houses may act upon it as a fact, that Mr. Greeley was not alive when the ballots were given." The two Houses separated. In this House, the honorable Senator from Vermont [Mr. EDMUNDS] proposed a resolution declaring that these four votes should not be counted. The Senator from Ohio before me [Mr. THURMAN] moved to amend by striking out the word "not," which amendment prevailed. I then moved an amendment, to add to the resolution, which then declared that those four undoubted votes for Mr. Greeley should be counted, words declaring the function of the two Houses in counting the votes to be ministerial as distinguished from the effect of that count or of those votes. Recently it has been stated that by this proposed amendment I had expressed the opinion that counting any votes, in any sense within the power of the two Houses, is purely ministerial! O, no, sir, I offered the amendment to have it appear that when the Senate said votes for a dead man should be counted, the Senate meant merely that being the votes of legal electors they should be enumerated, and announced, not that they should in legal effect be counted so that had there been a majority of votes for one dead it would follow that the Houses would ascertain and declare that a dead **man** should "fill the office of President of the United States." **While** these proceedings were progressing in this

Chamber, the House considered the four Georgia votes also. The House said the vote should not be counted at all in any sense, and so they were ignored and rejected. I refer to this to distinguish between counting the chairs in the Senate Chamber, and doing that which is involved in the constitutional direction touching the electoral votes. The word "count" does not govern so much as the words "the votes," the question always being what are "the votes" in the sense of the Constitution and of truth. The power which makes this determination is not technically judicial. Why? Because the question does not arise in a judicial proceeding. It is quasi judicial. It is the power to judge; it is the power to decide mixed questions of law and fact; it is the power, by judgment, to affirm truth and fact. The power to judge whether a bill shall pass or not, is not technically judicial; neither is it ministerial.

The power to pass on the validity and effect of electoral votes, is political: Yes, it is political; its exercise may involve the very highest attributes of sovereignty. When Colorado is reached, suppose a Member or Senator rises and says "I object to the votes of Colorado, because she is not a State in the Union." In the case of Colorado there is no doubt; but the question is the same as if she were shrouded in doubt. The question is, shall her vote be counted. The objection is that she is not a State in the Union, and the count or refusal to count her vote, is the only response to the objection. No higher political question can be solved or asked. Is she a State in law and in fact? Mr. President, nations have fought over that question for centuries. A State to-morrow may stand under the uplifted banners of revolt ; she may pass an ordinance of secession, prostrate all the forms of government, make treaties with foreign nations, seize the forts, arsenals, post-offices, custom-houses, dock-yards, and ships of the nation, and march an army into sister States. Shall her vote be counted? It is no answer to say, the law-making power may fix her status in advance. If her certificate is here, the question is, shall her votes be counted; and he who has the power to decide that question may decide it as he lists. The law-making power may have acted, or may have had no time to act, and what may be the force and effect of its action if it has acted, is only a factor in the open question.

Mr. EDMUNDS. An indeterminate one at that, on this theory.

Mr. CONKLING. Yes, an indeterminate one of course. A minority, but a considerable minority of the Law Committee of the House of Representatives is said to have reported that Colorado is not a State, that she is inchoate, inconsummate as a member of the Union, her statehood being in the chrysalis. Suppose, armed with this report, a member of the House objects to the count of Colorado's vote. The law-making power has acted, but the very question would be what is the force and effect of that action : and the Senator from Vermont may well say the action is indeterminate. If the Constitution reposes in you, sir, the prerogative and duty of determining what votes shall be counted, who are the members of the sisterhood of States by whom the Chief Magistrate is to be elected, whether you might weakly lean upon the opinion of somebody else or not, I will not consider ; but you and you alone at first and at last are to solve the question. Indeed, if I were to accept what was said by the Senator from Ohio [Mr. SHERMAN] this morning, I should begin to doubt myself whether my friends from Colorado are members of the Senate. I understood the Senator from Ohio to argue that the two Houses by law cannot enact in advance that on the happening of a certain contingency, a certain legal verity and conclusion shall become established. He stated that expressly, if I understood him aright. If that be true, awkward indeed would be the dilemma of Colorado. Congress, by an enabling act, authorized the then Territory of Colorado to assume statehood, the act declaring in advance that upon the happening of certain contingencies and proclamation thereof by the President of the United States, she should become crowned with statehood, with like force and effect as if she stood full-grown and proclaimed before the adoption of the act. The President has made that proclamation, evidential of that contingency; and the act of Congress, speaking afresh when the condition is complied with, Colorado is as complete in her rights as a member of the Union, as is the proudest or the most ancient State in all the sisterhood. But the Senator from Ohio disputes the doctrine by which she is here, and in so doing he confronts and combats the Supreme Court. That court long ago held in the embargo cases that such legislation in advance, incomplete, inconclusive, and inoperative, until the happening of an external contingency, is competent, and becomes effectual when the contingency occurs.

Mr. EDMUNDS. According to the judgment of the President of the United States.

Mr. CONKLING. And as my friend reminds me, the contingency resting on the action and judgment of the President of the United States.

But, Mr. President, I wander from the purpose. I had alluded to the proportions of questions lying within the power to decide whether electoral votes or alleged electoral votes shall or shall not be counted and made efficacious. I now maintain that the scope and vastness of this power, and of the questions and possibilities it may involve, are the measure of the certainty and clearness with which it must be conferred. Loose intendments will not do. Loose intendments may suffice for paltry uses; but in the last quarter of the nineteenth century loose intendments will not satisfy forty-five million free people that such supremacy resides in one functionary who may be made to-day by one majority of the votes in this single Chamber, and unmade to-morrow by the change of a single vote.

Do reason, and the fitness of things suggest that our fathers meant the President of the Senate should be the one man, even if there were to be one man, to decide whether alleged irregularity or fraud should vitiate the vote of a State, and turn the scale in the choice of Chief Magistrate of the Republic? Is such power so suited to one man, rather than to the American people in Congress assembled, that wisdom will extract it from words which drop him and turn away from him? The Constitution, speaking to you, Mr President, commands you in the presence of the States and of the people to produce and open all the certificates, and at that moment it turns its back on you. Will reason from such words, even if they be doubtful words, extract such transcendent prerogative, and repose it with him who is likely to sit as the sole judge in his own case?

Six times already, has the President of the Senate been one of the presidential candidates for or against whom the count was to be made. Was this not foreseen by the framers of the Constitution? The very men who drafted it proceeded in seven years to make the President of the Senate their own successful presidential candidate. And so, we are asked to believe that our fathers intended to make one individual the sole judge in his own case, though divine law and civilized jurisprudence had declared since the morning of time that no man should ever be judge in his own case, not even if other judges sat with him. In 1800 the authors of the Constitution, creating a committee of fifteen **to do what** the commission **now** proposed is to **do, provided** jealously **that** no candidate, and **no man** of kin to a candidate should be of the committee. The other day we had under consideration a constitutional amendment committing to nine judges holding their commissions for life, and as independent of parties and factions as is **the monarch** of the skies, the count of presidential **votes,** and it was there bluntly provided that not **one** of them should ever be eligible **as a** presidential candidate until after the **lapse of years.** This is **the** modern standard of safeguard against **self-interest.** Yet we are **asked** to believe that our fathers, trained **men,** the victims of **abuses under** other systems, and profoundly jealous as their words **and** acts show they were of the weakness the ambition and the greed of man, deposited absolute power with **a single individual to** decide for himself and for the nation whether **he should mount the highest** pinnacle of American if not of human **ambition.** They imposed no disability, or even interval of probation, on this **one judge, but straight-way** they made him the party also with their own **hands!** Such a **judge** we **are** invited to believe, they **so** intrenched, that in the presence of the whole **nation,** because in law every State and every citizen is present, he might by fraud or error undo the nation's will and the nation's right, and the nation must bow mute and helpless before wrong and usurpation. The courts of New Jersey, in accord with courts the world over, have lately said that no act of legislation can make a man judge in his own case, whether he sits alone or with other judges.

But we are warned that if the Houses have this power, they may baffle a count. They may throw out one State and another State until no majority of all the electors appointed remains. No doubt this is possible. Every page of the Constitution presents instances in which the two Houses, or one House alone, may defeat the Government. One House may refuse to pass appropriation bills, or tax bills, or army bills in war. The States may refuse to appoint electors or may appoint ineligible electors. The electors may refuse to vote or may vote for ineligible candidates. The President of the Senate may refuse to receive certificates, or refuse to open them, or refuse even to produce them. The governor of the State may refuse to certify or he may certify falsely. The Houses may refuse to attend, and so on. It all proves nothing. The answer Jefferson gave, "the Government rests on the consent of the governed." So must every free government rest while it stands at all, and whenever representatives and States and people forsake the government and leave it to languish and die, it will go down, as other governments have gone, to the sepulcher of blasted nationalities and buried epochs.

Is a majority less to be trusted than one man? A bare majority of one House may select a President of the Senate for the express, but secret purpose, of deciding a count and deciding it in a particular way. Is such a creature of an hour, doing the bidding of a bare majority of one House, more trustworthy than a majority of both Houses acting in the open light of day? Is the decision of one Senator in the case of Oregon, which decision might make him for one year or four years President of the United States, a stronger anchor for the nation than the decision of both Houses of Congress including that Senator, aided by the proposed tribunal in which five judges of the highest court must sit?

Mr. EDMUNDS. In a Republic.

Mr. CONKLING. Yes, and in this Republic, the only considerable experiment of free government extant on the globe—an experiment which, should it fail, would turn the clock of ages far back on the dial.

If the Constitution ordains this one-man power, let every man bow to it, mystery though it be. But I do not so read, I cannot so read. The canons of construction, the letter and spirit of the Constitution, reason, all revolt against a conclusion so puerile and so perilous. Prudence points with warning hand to a day when parties in the Senate may be reversed, and when new majorities may set up presiding officers to wield licentious power under a baneful precedent established now.

Thus far I have been indicating my own reasoning on the words employed. Let me now ascend to better reasoning. Let us inquire what has been done by illustrious men, sworn as we are sworn, to execute the Constitution. Let us survey the action of all the generations, and parties, and officials, who have proceeded under article 12, and also the action going before the Constitution and setting it in motion.

Reference has often been made to a resolution adopted by the constitutional convention in 1787. It has been cited as if it defined or construed the power we now consider. On the 17th of September, 1787, the constitutional convention adopted two resolutions. They were transmitted to the Congress of the Confederation. The Congress a few days afterward, on the 28th of September, accepted the report without acting upon it otherwise. These accompanying documents, and others, were sent to the States with the Constitution, and the Constitution was propounded to be ratified or rejected. One resolution recommended that the Senate should appoint a President for the sole purpose of opening and counting the electoral votes. Some observations may be made on this resolution in addition to those which fell from the Senator from Vermont.

In the first place the whole proceeding antedated the Constitution; it was before it was ratified; it was before it was proposed. Geologists would say it was prehistoric. It was a prefatory, or provisional proceeding. In the language of the resolution, "proceedings were to be commenced under the said Constitution." The ship was to be launched, and the launch might be by the sails or the machinery of the vessel, or by external and imparted force. It might be, as the French would say, by an impulsion: and those who made the launch chose so to make it. The resolution did not profess to define or construe any clause in the Constitution. It merely designated an occasion, and referred to the objects of that occasion. It did not even profess to conform to the modes which the Constitution would bring in. The Constitution directed that the electors should send their certificates to the President of the Senate. This resolution suggested that they should be sent to the Secretary of the United States. Who was he? He was the Clerk of the old Continental Congress. They had but one House and had a clerk, and this was the man. The resolution did not even propose that the counting should take place in the presence of the two Houses.

How did the Senate regard the action thus suggested.

George Washington had been unanimously chosen President. Every elector had voted for him. The electors themselves had been appointed with unanimity. Everybody from the beginning knew it would be so; it was matter of course. John Adams had been overwhelmingly elected Vice-President. To ascertain, the election, was a substantial and solemn proceeding, only as it is substantial and solemn for the Secretary of State to announce the Fourth of July, or a holiday.

The time to commence proceedings," according to the suggestion of the resolution, was March 4, 1789. Ten States had ratified the Constitution. A quorum of the Senate was 11. No quorum came to the seat of Government till April 6. Then no Senator was sworn in : it was January 3, 1790, before the oath of office was taken. Till then, there was no Senate and no Senator, but only Senators-elect. Ten months before they were sworn in as Senators, and on the 6th of April, 1789, eleven of those who afterward became Senators, proceeded to start the Government, and impart life and motion to the Constitution. They passed an order. Here it is :

Ordered, That Mr. Ellsworth inform the House of Representatives that a quorum of the Senate is formed; that a President is elected for the sole purpose of opening the certificates and counting the votes of the electors of the several States in the choice of a President and Vice-President of the United States ; and that the Senate is now ready, in the Senate Chamber, to proceed in the presence of the House to discharge that duty; and that the Senate have appointed one of their members to sit at the Clerk's table to make a list of the votes as they shall be declared ; submitting it to the wisdom of the House to appoint one or more of their members for the like purpose—who reported that he had delivered the message.

Had this order stopped midway, it might more plausibly be said to be a prescription or definition or expression of functions and powers. Even then I should deny that it was so; even then I should hold it merely to designate an occasion and purpose, not to determine or explain the part to be acted by each actor in the details of the transaction to take place. Let me illustrate my meaning : Suppose at the last session before the trial of an impeachment began, the Senate had adopted a resolution in these words "Ordered that Mr. Morrill be appointed President of the Senate for the sole purpose of trying the pending impeachment. Would such an order have implied that the President of the Senate so appointed was alone to conduct and determine the trial ? Certainly not. Why not? Because the Constitution does not so ordain. The Constitution states how much, and what he shall do, and therefore he could do no more, and it would be violent to suppose that the body adopting the order meant him to do anything save only that committed exclusively to him by law.

The governor of a State by order or proclamation appoints a particular judge to hold court for the sole purpose of trying an indictment for murder against A B. We do not understand such a proclamation to mean that the judge so appointed is himself alone to conduct the trial and decide the case. So, had the order of the Senate in question stopped with saying that John Langdon was elected solely for one purpose, I should understand it to mean that he was elected to act the part legally incumbent on him in the execution of that purpose, whatever it might be. I should understand the meaning and effect to be that he was not elected President of the Senate permanently, or generally, but that he was elected for one occasion only, or as lawyers would say *pro hac vice*.

But unfortunately, fatally I think, for the argument I am combating, the resolution does not stop with declaring that John Langdon was chosen only for a single purpose or occasion; it proceeds, "and that the Senate is now ready in the Senate Chamber to proceed in the presence of the House *to discharge that duty.*" The Senate is ready to discharge that duty. What duty ? Manifestly to count the votes, along with the House.

Mr. SARGENT. Why not "then open the certificates ?"

Mr. CONKLING. I thought I had assigned the reason. Because the Constitution declared who should open the certificates, and it declared that the President of the Senate should do it. In the distribution of duties, it reposed the duty to receive and open the cer-

2 CO

tificates, in the President of the Senate. It expressly gave this duty to him as his share and function in the transaction, and having done so, it abstained from giving him any other share or function. The Senate therefore in speaking of the duty reposed in itself and the House, did not speak of another duty expressly reposed in somebody else.

There is I think only one escape from this construction of the resolution and proceeding. We may escape it by saying that the proceeding being to inaugurate the Constitution, those who conducted it did not deem the Constitution yet operative, and therefore did not govern themselves by its mandates. If this be so, of course the argument sought from the occasion, favoring the power of the President of the Senate, falls to the ground.

The resolution proceeds further:

And that the Senate have appointed one of their members to sit at the Clerk's table, to make a list of the votes as they shall be declared—

And "declared" here I take it means "read" or "reported" or "announced."

submitting it to the wisdom of the House to appoint one or more of their members for the like purpose—

What did the House do? The House appointed a teller, and resolved that it would attend—

for the purpose expressed in the message delivered by Mr. Ellsworth.

I ask again what was that purpose? The House did attend. The tellers appointed by the two Houses made the enumeration of the votes. The Houses then separated. What next occurred? Mr. Madison came to the Senate to say that the House had directed him to inform the Senate that the House had agreed that the election should be certified or notified—now mark—" by such persons and in such manner as the Senate shall be pleased to direct." If the Constitution ordained that the President of the Senate should certify and declare the result, what had the House to do with it? What had the House to depute or concede to the Senate? What power could the Senate receive from the House? What could the Senate say or do in the matter, if the power and duty was lodged in the presiding officer? The Senate apparently thought however that it had everything to do with the affair after the House intrusted its part in it to the Senate.

A committee was appointed to prepare the certificates of election. One of the committee was Mr. Ellsworth and he had sat in the constitutional convention. The committee drew the certificate, and every word of it, and the President of the Senate was directed to sign it, and he did sign it. He signed it not of his own motion, or because authorized by the Constitution, but by the command of the Senate speaking for both Houses, and he signed it as the organ and mouthpiece of the two Houses.

The certificate recites that he who signed it had counted the votes. No doubt he counted them in the sense of arithmetic. Probably each of the other ten Senators did the like, the tellers surely did, but whatever they or the presiding officer did, was done by the assent and authority—nay by the command of the Houses. Had either teller been selected to sign the certificate, could he not have signed it with equal truth? Had the committee been directed to sign the certificate, would it not have been equally true as to those who signed it having counted the votes?

But now it is said that the certificate implies and proves that the

President of the Senate exercised the power, and the sole power to judge and determine what should be counted.

It is said, and truly, that afterward for many years the certificates used were in this ancient form. So they were. I ask the Senate to inquire whether they meant, or were intended to mean, that he who signed them had exercised the power to judge and determine.—I turn to 1805. Aaron Burr was President of the Senate. In his bad eminence as depicted by the Senator from Ohio, he was clear-headed and intrepid, and was never charged with being diffident of prerogative or distrustful of himself.

I ask the Senate to hear what Aaron Burr said when the electoral certificates were to be opened.

Mr. MORTON. From what does the Senator read?

Mr. CONKLING. I read from the compilation on page 36:

Mr. Burr stated that pursuant to law there had been transmitted to him several packets, which, from the indorsements upon them, appeared to be the votes of the electors of a President and Vice-President; that the returns forwarded by mail as well as the duplicates sent by special messengers had been received by him in due time.

From this point, observe his words. He was addressing the Senators and Representatives.

You will now proceed, gentlemen, said he, to count the votes as the Constitution and laws direct, adding that, perceiving no cause for preference in the order of opening the returns, he would pursue a geographical arrangement.

Turn now to the certificate of this count on the next page, page 37. There is the ancient form copied, "the undersigned certifies that he has counted the votes," although fresh on his lips were the words, preserved in the same record, that the Constitution committed it to the representatives of the States and the representatives of the people to conduct the count, and beside these words, is the attested fact that the count was actually conducted by the two Houses through their tellers. Turn to the proceedings in 1817. Indiana had entered the Union. Indiana was a State. Her Senators sat here, and in the House of Representatives sat William Hendricks, the ancestor of one of the recent candidates for Vice-President. Mr. Taylor from the State of New York when her certificate was read, rose and said "I object to that vote." It was alleged that Indiana less observant of right and truth than she is now, had cast out her shoe over certain territory not her own; that she had overreached and taken something from a sister-State; some other irregularities were laid at her door, and her votes were objected to. What occurred? Did the President of the Senate assume to determine? No, sir. Mr. Varnum, a Representative from New York,—and there was no twenty-second joint rule then,—Mr. Varnum moved that the Houses separate to decide whether the votes should be counted or not. The two Houses did separate; they did debate; they did consider. Nobody suggested that the President of the Senate had anything in the world to do with it; but yet in 1817, as usual, we find the certificate identical throughout with the earliest one. The tellers made the enumeration; the two Houses conducted the count; the President of the Senate did nothing, except what he was commanded to do; the two Houses prescribed the form of the certificate; they directed him to sign it and he did sign it, and the certificate stated that he counted the votes. No doubt he did in the arithmetical sense; he heard the tabulation read; he looked at it; he was convinced of the correctness of the enumeration; he announced it to the Houses. Again, see what John Adams stated on the 3d of February, 1797. Committees had been appointed, as they always were from 1793, beforehand, for what? "To ascertain and report the mode in which the electoral **vote** should be examined"—a bald usurpation, if the President of the Senate had the right to examine—they had reported directing the President of the Senate, to do certain things, one of which was on receiving **the** count from **the tellers** to declare the result. When Mr. Adams came to perform his duty, speaking on his oath, and speaking that the **nation might hear**, what did he say? That he derived his power from **the Constitution,** that the Constitution **conferred on** him this high **prerogative?** O, no, sir

In obedience to the Constitution and law of the United States and to the commands of both Houses of Congress expressed in their resolution passed at the present session, I now declare, et cetera.

At this point, as well as at any time, I may refer to a remark of Chancellor Kent, read yesterday by the Senator from Indiana, as if it were authority against the pending bill. This remark fell from the lips of the chancellor in one of the earlier addresses he made to college students. These lectures, when they began, were not designed as chapters of a law-book. Their author did not then know, that they were to be the germ of commentaries, which, growing in exactness and care, were to increase into one of the most famous and copious repositories of the law. They were designed originally to beguile the heaviness of unwonted and unwelcome leisure. The chancellor had left the bench at sixty, the constitutional limit; and as he says in some touching words which preface the earlier editions, he dreaded the heaviness of hours unemployed. He went into the **Columbia Law** School and held **discourse** mingled of history and jurisprudence, generalized **and** elementary dissertations designed to impart outlined instruction to beginners in the study of the law. I think **I must have borrowed some of his** words. Yes he says that "They are of that elementary kind which is not only essential to every person who pursues the science of the law as a practical profession, but is deemed useful and ornamental to gentlemen in every pursuit." Thus speaking to young men of affluence who were laying the foundations of culture at large, we observe that the language he employs is naturally inconclusive and regardless of judicial precision. What does he say:

In the case of questionable votes and a closely contested election, this power may be all-important.

That is, the power to count. I stop a moment to remind those who think that the count is mere arithmetic, of the condemnation of such a view involved in these words.

In the case of questionable votes and a closely contested election, this power may be all important.

I submit that if everything, good, bad, and indifferent, is as **we have been** told to be counted, **as the** multiplication table is said, there would be no "questionable votes," nor would the power **to** count, be "**all** important," or important at all. The sentence continues:

And I presume, in the absence of all legislative provision on the subject **that the** President **of** the Senate counts the votes and determines the result, and that the two Houses are present only as spectators to witness the fairness and **accuracy** of the transaction, and to act only if no choice be made by the electors.

These words suggest **three** observations.

"I presume." I need not ask lawyers whether that is the deliberate and considered phrase of a great magistrate long accustomed to weigh questions in **exact** scales and to pronounce distinctly and definitely his judgment upon them? "I presume" is not the language of judicial conclusiveness or exactness. O no.

Mr. EDMUNDS. It is a guess.

Mr. CONKLING. A guess, yes a guess—a pardonable form of speech when we remember the nature and object of the discourse. We next find these words: "In the absence of all legislative provision." Will any man who stands on the opinion of Chancellor Kent, after hearing these words, deny the power of the Houses to legislate? Or, to put the equivalent of the inquiry, will any man pretend in the face of these words that Chancellor Kent believed that the Constitution deposits with the President of the Senate this power?

If the Constitution in any way vests the power with the President of the Senate, that is the be-all and end-all of the matter; no legislative provision could touch it. If the chancellor believed the Constitution so provided, nothing could be more absurd than the words "in the absence of all legislative provision;" surely he knew that no legislative provision in such a case could have any more effect than the wind.

But again:

I presume in the absence of all legislative provision on the subject, that the President of the Senate counts the votes.

Yes, historically or in the sense of narrative he does; before these words were uttered by the chancellor nearly fifty years ago, historically and in the sense of narrative and in every sense essential to the truth of the statement, he did. So you, Mr. President, do a great many things, as your predecessors have done, by the acquiescence and command of the Houses. You appoint committees, not only of conference, but other committees. A standing rule of the Senate says the Senate shall appoint committees by ballot, does it not? But yet the President of the Senate appoints committees. How? He does it by the acquiescence of the body, as the organ of the body under the sanction of the body, just as he formerly signed the certificates to which I have referred.

In these instances the officer does not act in virtue of any right or power which inheres in him, independent of the Senate and its action conferring it.

The words of Chancellor Kent clearly indicate that in his opinion the examination of the electoral votes is within the law-making province. I beg to call attention to the view of the meaning of this passage from Kent, taken by others who are held in pleasant and respectful memory. In 1865 a warm debate over this clause of the Constitution occurred in the Senate. These words of Chancellor Kent were read, and Jacob Collamer of Vermont made some observations upon them. He said:

Nobody supposed that the Vice-President could exclude them.

That is, questioned votes—

But I was about to say that I never heard it doubted before that such a contingency, as might well happen because of the manner in which the constitutional provision was framed, could be provided for by legislation. Chancellor Kent, in the first volume of his Commentaries, says.

And then he quotes. Mr. Collamer resumes.

He admits that it is in the power of Congress to legislate, and doubts only whether in the absence of legislation there exists any department of the Government or any officer of the Government vested with power to count the votes and declare the result; and in relation to that he is only able to bring himself to state by way of opinion that he presumes the President of the Senate is to count the votes and declare the result. But he presumes that only in the absence of legislation. Legislation on the subject, therefore, according to the high authority of this distinguished jurist, is admissible, and of course within the power of Congress.

My eye falls here, Mr. President, on words uttered by your predecessor, Jacob M. Howard of Michigan, then a Senator, whose attainments

as a lawyer were recognized by **all who** knew him, who **was** one of
the leaders of the republican party, and who believed, **and** as you
believe and as I believe in that party, in its usefulness and its mis-
sion, and in its record, resplendent as it is beyond any **other** in ardu-
ous and illustrious achievements. Mr. Howard said :

I confess I do not doubt the power of Congress, should they see fit, **to** authorize
the President of the Senate to count the votes after he has opened the certificates;
but in the absence of such a statutory provision I certainly could not concur in the
"presumption" of Chancellor Kent, that the President of the Senate would have
the right to count the votes and declare the result. It is impossible for me to concur in this intimation of that very distinguished authority. I should on the contrary, hold, in the absence of an act of Congress, that the duty of counting the votes
devolved on the two Houses of Congress thus assembled.

Mr. President, I have paused at the resolution **of 1787 and** the **proceeding** of 1789, at the form of certificate **then and** long afterward
used, and at the remark **of** Chancellor Kent, **because** these make up
the trio of authorities usually cited of late to **support** the theory that
the President of the Senate is **appointed by the Constitution** to con-
duct the electoral count.

I come now to review **the practice of the nation for eighty-three
years—from 1793 to 1877.**

Until 1869, **beginning in** 1793, as often as electoral votes were to be
counted, committees were raised by each House in advance to ascertain **and** report **the** mode in which the votes should be examined.
The committees reported how the proceeding should be conducted, the
report was adopted by each House, and one thing always provided
for, was the appointment of tellers by **each House.**

The right of the Houses thus asserted, was never questioned. No
President of the Senate, **no member** of either House, ever interposed
a challenge. When **the day** to open the certificates arrived, the **two**
Houses directed the proceeding throughout. The tellers **counted.**
Every question which **arose** was referred to the Houses. The **Houses**
framed the certificate ; they directed **it to be signed.** He who signed
it was the **organ** and representative **of the two Houses.**

January 24.

Mr. CONKLING. **Mr. President,** I tried yesterday to answer in part
the chief objection to the pending bill. That objection had then re-
ceived little attention in the Senate. The honorable Senator from Cali-
fornia has this morning given it the weight of his authority. Senators
have asked why I devoted so much pains yesterday to disproving the
authority of the President of the Senate, saying that nobody in the
Senate contends for such a power, or believes it to exist. The Senator
from California is I believe its only known advocate in the Senate ; but
nevertheless the chief objection to the pending bill prevailing in the
press and in the country at large, is the idea that the Constitution clothes
the President of the Senate with power to do whatever can be done in
deciding on and making effectual electoral votes, and in judging con-
flicting certificates. If this objection be well founded, the bill has
no footing. I dwelt yesterday on the text of the Constitution to show,
first, that it does authorize the President of the Senate to receive, keep,
and produce and **open** all the certificates ; and that the Constitution
does not empower him **after** they are opened to pass on the votes they
may contain second, that implication works power to do only those
things incident and essential to an expressly authorized act, and that
when the expressly authorized act is done and ended, implication stops.

From this I had **argued** that as **the** opening of sealed certificates must take place before the votes they contained can be examined or touched, and of course before counting can begin, the power to open beforehand, cannot imply the power to do a separate, a different, a greater thing, afterward.

I referred to the fact that every count from the beginning has been conducted and controlled by the two Houses, that from first to last tellers appointed by the Houses have enumerated, and that the President of the Senate has never even enumerated the votes; that the certificate reciting the count has been framed and ordered by the two Houses and signed by the President of the Senate as their organ expressly authorized and commanded to sign it; that the form of the certificate remained identical from the beginning, and was used and signed on occasions when we know that the Houses entertained objections to votes, and when the record shows conclusively that the certificate did not and could not imply any power assumed by the President of the Senate of himself to determine anything touching the electoral votes.

Allusion should have been made to the further fact that in no instance has the President of the Senate assumed to judge or to decide anything, or to do anything beyond opening the packets, except by the command of the two Houses. Georgia's vote in 1800 having been brought into the Senate this morning as it has been sometimes brought in before, I turn aside to remark that if the name of Jefferson is liable to injury now because of a suspicion that taking up a paper void of form and void of substance as a constitutional certificate, he silently in his seat induced the tellers, notwithstanding its latent and its patent vice, to count it for him; if, I say, the memory of Jefferson be exposed to such aspersion, it is exposed to serious aspersion indeed.—He was acting as the organ and agent of the two Houses, in their presence, authorized by their acquiescence, and the intimation is that he proceeded to do clandestinely something not revealed to them, and something by the clear mandate of the resolutions under which the Houses were proceeding, not within his province, and something the success of which depended on secrecy and concealment from the Houses.

If such a thing were supposable in the case of Jefferson, what a light it casts on the danger of trusting one man in such a matter, and what a satire it is on the notion that the Houses can be effectual witnesses knowing and verifying the truth, and yet leaving the whole matter in the keeping of the presiding officer.

I alluded yesterday to the fact that always till 1869, committees have been appointed to pre-arrange the process of verifying and ascertaining the result of presidential elections. This practice never ceased till the twenty-second joint standing rule was made in 1865. That rule has gone. The custom of raising committees to ascertain and report the mode of determining the result, has revived. Committees have been appointed, the report of the committees is the pending bill which awaits the action of the Senate, and the question is whether we are to have that method, or no method, or some other method not suggested and which no time remains to devise.

I now beg the attention of the Senate to a chapter of history. It begins in 1800. The Constitution was then ten years old. The men who devised it were still in the vigor of life, and the nation confided in them, and leaned on them. Many of them sat in Congress, for years. Among these men was James Madison. He has been called the father of the Constitution; a few years later he became President of the United States. The Constitution on its face had specified five instances in which votes could not make a man President of the United

States. Five disabilities were imposed upon the presidential office. One disability was imposed on the office of presidential elector. All this was true when the Constitution was launched in 1789. It has been said in this debate that the ken of man, the forecast of sages, did not in the beginning discern the possibility that serious problems might require solution in the count and ascertainment of electoral votes. I ventured yesterday to deny the assertion. I repeat the denial now. In 1796 a presidential election had been held ; electors had been appointed by the States, Vermont among them. Madison and Jefferson, separated by distance, were in correspondence, and Madison wrote to Jefferson that the election was still in doubt—this was weeks after the electors had been appointed,—because of the allegation that there was " vice. (I use his word) in the vote of Vermont. He wrote that if her electoral votes turned out to be valid, the election would be one way, otherwise it might be the other way. What was the vice, or alleged vice, in the vote of Vermont ? The State of Vermont was then living under a constitution wanting in provision for the choice of electors, no statute had been passed directing the mode in which electors should be appointed, and the Constitution of the United States ordained that they should be appointed by the States in the mode directed by their Legislatures. The Legislature of Vermont, in the absence of a statute, proceeded itself to appoint electors. That was the customary mode observed then in other States, except in those in which the governor alone appointed. Argument arose. On the one side it was said " the Legislature of Vermont has not directed the mode in which presidential electors shall be appointed ; there is no statute ; and the Legislature can speak only by statute." On the other hand it was said " when the Legislature proceeds itself to choose electors, does it not direct the process ? Does it not say, by action speaking louder than words, how the electors shall be chosen." And it was of that doubt, and of the " vice" it suggested, that James Madison, on the 25th of December 1796 wrote to Thomas Jefferson these words :

I cannot entirely remove the uncertainty in which my last left the election. Unless the Vermont election, of which little has of late been said, should contain some fatal vice in it, Mr. Adams may be considered as the Pres.dent-elect.

Two weeks afterward, on the 8th of January, 1797, he wrote :

If the Vermont votes be valid, as is now generally supposed, Mr. Adams will have 71 and you 68, Pinckney being in the rear of both.

Mr. President, these letters were written very soon after the Constitution first spoke ; they are not the letters of one who was startled and amazed that such a question should arise, and who knew of no way in which it could be solved—the whole manner indicates quite the opposite. Other facts might be cited—the receipt in Congress of petitions from New England charging wrong in the appointment of electors, and not alone such petitions, to show that, immediately after the adoption of the Constitution, and, as I insist by reason of what appears even on its face, before its adoption, its authors foresaw that questions might arise requiring the power of deciding and judging the result of presidential elections.

Coming to the year 1800, I hold up the plain evidence that of both Houses of Congress, and the leaders of thought in the country, had their attention sharply fixed on the necessity of providing for the adjudication of some at least of the very questions involved in the count of votes which now awaits us.

On the 23d of January, 1800, Mr. Ross in the Senate moved a committee to " inquire whether any and what provision should be made touching disputed elections."—I quote the language—"disputed elections of President and Vice-President of the United States." It was the 14th of February before report was made. It was the 28th of March before the bill reported was finally acted upon; and the interval is dotted on the skeleton record which has come down to us with the days and occasions on which the Senate, and afterward the House, bestowed upon it most earnest consideration. In the House the bill was managed and the debate was led by John Marshall, who had already given evidence of those remarkable and rugged powers, and of that thorough knowledge of the elements of the Constitution, which were so soon to select him as the head of the new nation's highest court. A year later he became Chief-Justice, and at once he began to fill all lands with his renown as a jurist and a statesman. It is said that at the age of twenty-seven Edward Coke was the greatest common lawyer in the world. As truly has it been said that John Marshall was as great a master of our Constitution as ever lived. I have words of his to read to the Senate. The bill, which I will presently refer to more at large, had passed the Senate; it was pending in the House in Committee of the Whole. Its title was "A bill prescribing the mode of deciding disputed elections for President and Vice-President." Here is the record:

The bill having been read, and the first section being under consideration, Mr. Marshall, after speaking of the importance of the subject before the committee—

The Committee of the Whole House—

and the necessity—

I beg Senators to observe this—

and the necessity of some salutary mode being adopted for this object—

That is to settle disputed elections of President and Vice-President—

expressed his doubts of the propriety of two points in this first section of the bill, to-wit: first, that the Senate were to name the chairman of the grand committee, and secondly that the opinion of this grand committee was to be final. He therefore moved to strike out of the section so much as related to those principles, and read what he wished to introduce for a substitute.

Here is an explicit statement both of the power of Congress to legislate, and of the "necessity" of adopting a "salutary mode" of conducting the count, and deciding disputes. I will presently show what Marshall deemed a "salutary mode." Before doing so however, I wish to advert to a statement made yesterday by the Senator from Ohio [Mr. SHERMAN.] He said Mr. Pinckney, Charles Pinckney, then a Senator, answered the arguments made in favor of the now pending bill. Did the Senator mean to lead the Senate to believe that Charles Pinckney or any other man who took part in the debate of 1800, intimated that an ounce of power, a feather's weight of authority, a particle of prerogative resided with the President of the Senate to judge an electoral vote or to determine the result of a presidential election? Here is the argument of Charles Pinckney. I infer that, after the manner of later times, it was a verbally-prepared argument; it would so seem, because in this book and its fellow-volumes, "the Annals of Congress," it appears as one of the rare instances in which, in extenso, any man is reported, and short-hand writers did not exist then. I think I have a right to suppose that Mr. Pinckney was reported by himself. I will read a few of his words; the honorable Senator from California also made allusion to Mr. Pinckney.

It is made their duty—

That is the duty of the two Houses—

It is made their duty to count over the votes in a convention of both Houses, and for the President of the Senate to declare who has the majority of the **votes of elect-** ors transmitted.

Again :

From this part of the Constitution it is evident that no power or authority is given to Congress, even when both Houses are assembled in convention, further than to open and to count the votes, and declare who are President and Vice-President, if an election has been made ; but if no election has been made, &c.

I do not read these passages **as contributions to the argument that more** or less power resides in **the two Houses. I read it merely to** show how far it was from **the purpose of Mr. Pinckney to assert any** prerogative for the President **of the Senate. His argument was quite** different. The argument was **that the electors were to be appointed** by the States, that this was the **function and attribute of the States,** and that nothing was to be done by the two **Houses, or by anybody,** except to ascertain **what the** States had done. **And I beg just here, to** say that **I do not believe** any Senator who **concurred in reporting the** bill **now** before **the Senate** holds any other doctrine.

To ascertain **the act of** the States, is the whole object of **the** bill. **The sole inquiries authorized** by the bill are, did the State appoint **electors, who are they, how** did they vote. These inquiries answered, **the proceeding is ended,** whether the State be New York or Louisiana. **There is the mete and bound** which **no** power can lawfully overpass. **Whoever treads beyond, will** trample on the Constitution, and at**tempt to establish brute force or** partisan fraud **on** the ruins of law.

Charles Pinckney said it was for the States to appoint electors **; the electors were to speak, and then, with a** confidence **which a** longer **life would have shaken, he added, Who can suppose that any** State **will ever attempt to make an office-holder an elector, or will** ever do any **other thing which the Constitution forbids ?** If I were to say that **he argued that the whole subject must be left** literally to the States, **I should overstate him. His argument** was **that** it had better be so **left, that it** was not **worth while to be** pragmatic, nor to anticipate **difficulties or** problems, **but rather to** trust to the placid promise of a **hopeful** by **and by :** better **to** trust **that** all the States, observing the **Constitution,** would speak and act according to **it.** He said that **no irregularity** had then occurred, and that he believed no dispute about **the election would ever come** to vex the ear of Congress, **or of the nation.**

He said also that Congress had nothing to do with electing a President in the first instance, but he did not say that Congress had nothing to do with finding out who the people in the States had elected,

No, sir, he said nothing of the sort, nor did he intimate that whatever was to be done in ascertaining the result of presidential elections, should or could be done by the President of the Senate, or by anybody except Congress.

At the end of the argument of Mr Pinckney the Senate passed the bill. Here it is. As reported by the committee in the Senate it provided that of the committee, the "grand committee," as it was called, to be created, the Chief-Justice should be chairman. The honorable Senator from Ohio [Mr. SHERMAN] was right yesterday in saying that the Chief-Justice was stricken out. I ask the attention of the Senator from California [Mr. SARGENT] to the amendment by which the Chief-Justice was dispensed with. In lieu of the provision that the Chief-Justice should be chairman of the grand committee, was inserted this provision :

It shall be the duty of the Senate and House of Representatives of **the United** States to draw by lot in each House six members thereof.

I can state more briefly than I can read the residue of the amendment. By lot six members were to be drawn. Three were to be selected from the six, and of these three a chairman of the committee was to be found. There are several other provisions to which I ask attention. The title of the bill I have already indicated. Section first provided for the constitution of a committee to be known as a grand committee, and I ask Senators to observe the power given to it :

And shall have power to examine and finally to *decide all disputes relative to the election of President and Vice-President of the United States: Provided always,* That no person shall be deemed capable of serving on this committee, who is one of the five highest candidates, or of kin to any of the five highest candidates.

Section 3 :

Each House shall then proceed to choose, by ballot, two members thereof as tellers, whose duty it shall be to receive *the certificates of the electors from the President of the Senate, after they shall have been opened and read.*

Each member of the committee was to take and subscribe an oath, and to that oath I also call attention. The oath was—

I will impartially examine the votes given by the electors of President and Vice-President of the United States, *together with all the exceptions and petitions against them,* and a true judgment give thereon according to the evidence.

Section 4 provides :

The President of the Senate shall then deliver to the chairman **of** the grand committee all the certificates **of** the electors, and all the certificates or other documents transmitted by them, or by the executive authority of any State, and all the petitions, exceptions. and memorials against the votes of the electors, or the persons for whom they have voted, together with the testimony accompanying the same.

The Senator from Ohio observed. erroneously, yesterday, that the pending bill provides for a secret session of the commission. Not so. This bill of 1800 made that provision. I will read it :

They shall sit with closed doors. and a majority of the members may proceed to act, provided the number from each House is equal.

But for an unwillingness to consume the time of the Senate I would stop to remind the Senator from California how our fathers thought that impartiality might be gained by counterpoising against each other opposing predilections. One House at that time was largely federal ; the other was largely republican ; divided somewhat as the Houses are divided now, and this scheme provided that the committee to be composed of both Houses should act only when each House was represented with exact equality. Section 6 provided :

That the grand committee shall have *power to send for persons, papers and records, to compel the attendance of witnesses, to administer oaths to all persons examined before them, and to punish contempts of witnesses refusing to answer.*

Section 8 :

That the grand committee shall have power to inquire, examine, decide **and report**, upon the constitutional qualifications of the persons voted for as President and Vice-President of the United States ; upon the constitutional qualifications of the electors appointed by the different States, and whether their appointment was authorized by the State Legislature or not ; upon all petitions and exceptions against corrupt, illegal conduct of the electors, or **force**. menaces **or improper means** used to influence their votes ; **or against the truth of their returns,** or the time, **place or** manner of giving their votes.

Section 10 : the report of a majority of the said committee shall be a final and conclusive determination of the admissibility, or inadmissibility, of the votes given by **the** electors for President and Vice-President of the United States : and where votes are rejected by the grand committee, their reasons shall be stated in writing for such exclusion.

This bill being amended in several particulars, but in no particular changing the provisions which I have recited, save only to exchange the Chief-Justice as chairman for a chairman to be obtained by lot, passed the Senate by a decided majority.

Mr. SARGENT. By a majority of 4.

Mr. CONKLING. Sixteen to twelve. Sixteen to twelve was a decided majority in a body so small. It passed the Senate after a vigorous and pertinacious opposition never for one moment grounded upon the idea, never in any instance suggesting the idea, that the power whatever it might be, to ascertain presidential elections, did not reside in the two Houses, or that any power touching the subject did reside in the President of the Senate, beyond opening the certificates.

It is to be observed that receiving, keeping and opening such documents, is not a duty of that paltry or menial nature described by the Senator from California when he spoke of "a common carrier of papers." It is a duty of honor and solemnity. It is to receive in trust, and in high trust, the secret certificates of what has been done by bodies of men in great matters, and to preserve them inviolate until in the presence of the representatives of States and the representatives of the people, and invested with more than the interest heirs feel when, in homely phrase, a will is opened, for the first time the whole nation and the world may know what has been consummated by the average and aggregated judgment of all the States. This is no undignified affair—it is not beneath a sovereign. Be this function great or petty, never was it hinted in the debate of 1800 that any power inhered in the presiding officer to judge of anything.

Now I call attention to an amendment offered in the Senate by Mr. Nicholas. If distinguished for no other reason, this amendment will be heard with respect because it commanded not only the preference but the approbation of Thomas Jefferson. Those who have read his letters written at the time will remember that he says, everything offered by a republican is voted down by the customary majority of two to one: but he says in a few days an amendment will be offered which will express the republican view. Here is that amendment. I am not going to read the whole of it. Its chief feature, and that which commanded the approval of Mr. Jefferson, was that when objection was made to a vote, that objection was to be passed upon by the two Houses sitting in joint meeting and voting *en masse* and *per capita*, Senator by Senator and Member by Member. That was the theory Mr. Jefferson held. It found expression in this amendment, and the preamble of the amendment is interesting for other reasons. I ask the Secretary to read it.

The Secretary read as follows:

Amendments to the bill prescribing the mode of deciding disputed elections of President and Vice-President of the United States.

Strike out the ten first sections, and insert:

Whereas, in an election of President and Vice-President of the United States, questions may arise, whether an elector has been appointed in a mode authorized by the Legislature of his State or not? Whether the time at which he was chosen, and the day on which he gave his vote were those determined by Congress? Whether he were not at the time, a Senator or Representative of the United States, or held an office of trust or profit under the United States? Whether one at least, of the persons he has voted for, is an inhabitant of a State other than his own? Whether the electors voted by ballot, and have signed, certified and transmitted to the President of the Senate, a list of all the persons voted for; and the number of votes for each? Whether the persons voted for are natural-born citizens, or were citizens of the United States, at the time of the adoption of the Constitution, were thirty-five years old, and had been fourteen years resident within the United States? And the Constitution of United States having directed that the President of the Senate shall—

Mr. CONKLING. Now I beg the Senate to listen to the words about to be read.

The Secretary continued to read, as follows:

Having directed that the President of the Senate shall, in the presence of the Senate and House of Representatives, open all the certificates, and that the votes shall then be count-

ed, from which the reasonable inference and practice has been, that they are to be counted by the members composing the said Houses and brought there for that office, no other being assigned them; and inferred the more reasonably as thereby the constitutional weight of each State in the election of those high officers, is exactly preserved in the tribunal which is to judge of its validity, the number of Senators and Representatives from each State, composing the said tribunal, being exactly that of the electors of the same State.

SECTION 1. Be it enacted, &c.. That whensoever the members of the Senate and House of Representatives shall be assembled for the purpose of having the certificates of the electors of the several States opened and counted, the names of the several States shall be written on different and similar tickets of paper, and put into a ballot-box out of which one shall be drawn one at a time—

Mr. CONKLING. That is enough. I do not wish to shock the tender sensibilities of the Senate by making them hear that their fathers proposed to toss a penny or draw anything out of a ballot-box. They did, however, provide that the President of the Senate should not even determine for himself the order in which he would pick up and break the seals of these packets. They provided that putting in a box a paper each containing the name of a State, a member of one House should shake the box and a member of the other House should draw out a paper; and then the President of the Senate should open the certificate indicated by the lot, and no other, and that until every exception taken to the votes of that State was adjudged and acted upon, no other certificate should be opened. But all this involved the doctrine of chance, and in the gladsome light of these better days who would be a dark idolator of chance. O no: not we: not we, who are endowed with scruples and virtues which our fathers never knew. This amendment offered in the Senate failed. It failed not because of its preamble but because of the latter part of its substance, which I will read:

The packet containing the certificates of that State, shall be opened by the President of the Senate, and shall then be read, and then shall be read also the petitions, depositions and other papers and documents concerning the same, and if no exception is taken thereto, the votes contained in such certificate shall be counted, but if the votes or any of them shall be objected to,—

Now comes the not acceptable provision—

the members present shall, on the question propounded by the President of the Senate, decide, without debate, by yea or nay, whether such votes or vote are constitutional or not, and the votes of one State being thus counted, another ticket shall be drawn from the ballot-box.

It will be perceived these latter words required a call of the roll in the joint meeting in which every Senator as a unit, and every member as a unit, should respond yea or nay. Naturally enough the States would not surrender their preponderance of power in the Senate, and would not consent to having Senators merged with the more numerous House of Representatives; and therefore the Senate rejected this amendment; I repeat, the blunt recital in the preamble, that the power was with the Houses and none of it with the presiding officer, received no criticism in either House.

In the House the bill was reported with amendments not one of which bears upon the topic we are now considering. The two Houses differed, and the bill was rent on a rock. One House was republican in its majority, and the other was federal. It was said in one House that if either House decided against the count of an electoral vote it should be cast out; in the other House it was insisted that no vote should be cast out unless both Houses so said; and accordingly on the word "admit" or the word "reject" the Houses differed. They first insisted; they then adhered, in parliamentary parlance; and the bill fell, because a political party in the Senate would not yield into the hands of a political party in the House, the *jus disponendi* of an electoral vote; but all men, and both parties, and both Houses, concurred in affirming by words and by votes that it was for the two Houses of Congress as such, or for the law-making power to conduct, and conclude the ascertainment of electoral votes.

No one disputed this position.

Mr. President, begging pardon for occupying so much time upon the bill of 1800 which contained nearly every essential element, certainly every one to which most serious objection is made, to be found in the bill before us, I beg to ask attention to the legislation of 1824. Objection had been made to the count of the vote of Indiana in 1817. Missouri had put into her constitution, touching free men of color, provisions obnoxious to a large portion of the nation, and objection had been made to the count of her vote. In 1824 in the Senate came forward Martin Van Buren, the organ of the Committee on the Judiciary of the Senate. He came forward in response to a resolution passed on the 16th of December, 1823, a resolution which summoned that committee to ascertain and report what, in regard to the count of electoral votes, the public interest and the public safety required. On the 4th of March he reported the bill which I hold in my hand. Not until the 19th of April and after much debate and consideration did it pass the Senate. It went to the House and was referred to the Judiciary Committee on the 21st of April, 1824. It was reported back in the House from the Judiciary Committee, unanimously as far as the record shows. Who reported it? Who was the organ of the Law Committee in the House when this bill was reported? Daniel Webster, of Massachusetts. He reported it without changing the dot of an *i* or the cross of a *t*. No amendment or cavil was suggested. It had passed this body. It had been managed here by Mr. Van Buren who soon afterward led his party in the national canvass, and stood the acknowledged and visible head of the democratic church; and Mr. Van Buren was a lawyer of no mean attainments. It was reported in the House with approval by Mr. Webster, who was known as the great expounder of the Constitution, but it was not reported until the 10th of May, 1824. It was then referred to the Committee of the Whole, and when the 10th of May has arrived in this latitude, the House of Representatives and the Senate have approached the term of the session. The Houses adjourned, and thus the bill was lost. I turn to two of its provisions. It provides, curiously enough, that on the first occasion when the votes were to be counted the joint meeting should be held in the Hall of the House, and on after occasions the two Houses should assemble in the Rotunda.

The Senate and House of Representatives shall meet in the Hall of the House of Representatives at the next occasion, and on all future occasions in the center room of the Capitol.

That I take it be the Rotunda. They were to meet under **the Dome of the** Capitol on neutral ground between the two Halls.

The bill provides that at twelve o'clock of the day appointed for the counting of the votes, the two Houses shall meet as I have described.

The packet containing the certificates from the electors of each State shall then be opened by the President of the Senate, beginning with the State of New Hampshire—

And going through **the** States geographically—

and if no exceptions are taken thereto, all the votes contained in such certificates shall be counted; but, if any exception be taken, the persons taking the same shall state it in writing, directly, and not argumentatively, and sign his name thereto—and if the exception be seconded, &c.

I pass over that:

And then each House shall immediatly retire, without question or debate, to its own department, and shall take the question on the exception, without debate, by ayes and noes. So soon as the question shall be taken in either House, a message shall be sent to the other informing them—

Of what?

informing them of the decision of the question and that the House sending the message is prepared to resume the count.

Not to resume witnessing a count to be conducted by somebody else, but to resume the count,

and when such message shall have been received by both Houses, they shall again meet in the same room as before, and the count shall be resumed. And if the two Houses have concurred in rejecting the vote or votes objected to, such vote or votes shall not be counted; but unless both Houses concur, such vote or votes shall be counted.

That, Mr. President, was the bill of 1824. Be it wise or unwise, it asserts again by a unity of voices with no recorded doubt, that the paramount law had reposed in the two Houses the duty, and commanded them to see to it, that constitutionally, lawfully, and truly, the result of presidential elections should be ascertained.

I have said that in 1817 the vote of Indiana was challenged. Her Senators sat in the Senate Chamber. In the House also she was represented. The question was shall this vote be counted? The Houses separated, entertained the objection, and deliberated.

In 1821 Missouri had come in. Before the day to count arrived on a motion made in either House a committee was appointed to consider and forecast the disposition to be made of an anticipated objection. Just here it may be well to notice a suggestion we have sometimes heard. It is said that it is impracticable for the two Houses to attempt to decide objections to votes when the count takes place; because if they have the legal power they have not the time to make the inquiry. Why is there not time? Why, because the second Wednesday in February is the day for the count to begin, and the interval before the 4th of March is too brief to permit inquiry. The first answer to this suggestion is that the day is fixed only by statute, and can be changed to a day early enough to leave ample time. The pending bill does change the day, so as to avoid insufficiency of opportunity. But the other answer is suggested by the case of Missouri and by other instances in which dispute has arisen. The fact is always known in advance, as in the present instance it has been known, that objections of particular kinds will arise in regard to particular States, and this enables each House to inquire seasonably, as each House has done now, into the grounds of the anticipated objection.

It was in this way that Mr. Clay was enabled to move a committee in 1821 in the House, and to come to a resolution with a Senate committee prescribing in advance exactly what should be done with the vote of Missouri. The order of the Houses, thus made beforehand, was that the vote should be reported thus: if the votes be counted, the count will stand so and so, if not counted, so and so, but in either case James Monroe has received a majority of all the electors appointed, and is therefore President of the United States.

In effect the votes were rejected.

No suggestion was made that the presiding officer had any power over the question. I measure my expression in saying no power, because he was Vice-President, and not even a member of this body, and had not even a vote, except in the case of a tie. If he had been as you are, Mr. President, a member of the Senate, he would have had a vote. You have a vote not qua your Presidency of the Senate, but qua your

Senatorship. It is because you hold the credentials of the great State of Michigan as a Senator, and not because I had the pleasure of voting for you along with a majority of Senators to preside over us, that you have a vote and thereby one-seventy-fifth of the power of the Senate.

In 1837 the vote of Michigan was dealt with by the Houses, as Missouri had been thirteen years before.

In 1857 the certificate of Wisconsin was opened. A snow-storm had raged in Wisconsin. The electors were impeded in reaching Madison, the capital of that State. They arrived at Madison a day too late. The law said they must vote the day before. The question was, is the law in this respect mandatory or is it merely directory? James M. Mason of Virginia sat in your chair. The Houses met, to count the vote. Wisconsin's certificate was reached. Objection was made. The presiding officer said "this is not the time." The tellers wrote upon their table. The objection was insisted on. Mr. Mason said— I state it briefly, not wishing to dwell upon it, but I mean to state it accurately, and I invite review and correction if I am wrong—the President of the Senate said, "no proceeding is in order here, the two Houses sitting together, which requires debate or a vote here. That, I rule as the presiding officer of these two bodies," as he was by the by, not because he was President of the Senate. No, Sir John Randolph early raised his voice against that idea; but because of the comity and agreement of the two Houses he was selected for that occasion to act as the moderator or presiding officer of the joint meeting. Mr. Mason ruled that nothing was in order there which involved debate or a vote in the two Houses sitting together. One of the tellers, Mr. Jones, of Tennessee, rose, as the record will show, and said I take it the true mode is for the Houses to separate and determine separately whether this vote shall be counted or not. Mr. Mason rose, I use his words now, and said, "the Chair so considers." During the proceeding, in every form of convenient words, he disclaimed all power. He said in substance I have no power to count this vote or to refuse to count it. I have no power to say it is a good vote or a bad vote. My business is to open the certificates. I do it. The two Houses must decide whether the vote is constitutional and can be counted or not. Stephen A. Douglas of Illinois then a Senator, broke into a somewhat violent, I prefer to say impassioned exclamation, and yet scarcely more impassioned than that in which John J. Crittenden expressed himself, and it may be said of him that the snows of seventy winters on his head never quenched the fires of patriotism that glowed beneath. He and Douglas and others rose and said, "I protest; I record my protest against the idea that the presiding officer has anything to do, even by ruling a question of order, with putting a curb or bit upon proceedings here." The President of the Senate again disclaimed all intention to influence the proceedings. On the motion of a Senator the Houses separated. The Senate came here and debate took place, and again the presiding officer washed his hands and purged himself of what he said would have been an attempt at usurpation, saying that he had nothing to do with the matter except to open the certificates, and then as authorized by the two Houses to act as the presiding officer of the joint meeting; but the Houses, and they alone, must determine whether a vote was good, or whether it was bad, or he might have added whether it was indifferent; an inquiry which would have been quite immaterial if the law had been, as announced here the other day, that no matter whether good, bad, or indifferent, in either alternative equally, votes are to be counted.

I come now to a resolution adopted by the two Houses in 1865, after much debate in the Senate. Rebellion stood with gory and uplifted hand. I will admit for the sake of the argument, or rather I shall not read the resolution to dispute, that acts might be proper in the presence of such events, which in their absence would have been without justification, possibly without extenuation.

Mr. HOWE. The Senator admits it?

Mr. CONKLING. I admit it for the sake of the argument. I affirm nothing in regard to it. I never believed the Constitution was violated by asserting that the Government had the right to be. I never believed it was violated because it was asserted that the nation had authority by the beak and claw to put down rebellion. Here is the resolution:

Be it resolved by the Senate and House of Representatives of the United States of America in Congress assembled, That the States mentioned in the preamble to this joint resolution are not entitled to representation in the electoral college for the choice of President and Vice-President of the United States for the term of office commencing on the 4th day of March, 1865—

Now—

and no electoral votes shall be received or counted from said States concerning the choice of President and Vice-President for said term of office.

Approved February 8, 1865.

That resolution went to Mr. Lincoln, the President of the United States. Hear what Mr. Lincoln said:

The joint resolution entitled, &c., has been signed by the Executive—

I am reading the language of Abraham Lincoln—

has been signed by the Executive, in deference to the view of Congress implied in its passage and presentation to him. *In his own view, however, the two Houses of Congress concur under the twelfth article of the Constitution—*

Not the twenty-second joint rule,—that rule did not then exist—

have complete power to exclude from counting all electoral votes deemed by them to be illegal; and it is not competent for the Executive to defeat or obstruct that power by a veto, as would be the case if his action were at all essential in the matter. He disclaims all right of the Executive to interfere in any way in the matter of canvassing or counting the electoral votes, and he also disclaims that by signing said resolution he has expressed any opinion on the recitals of the preamble, or any judgment of his own upon the subject of the resolution.

ABRAHAM LINCOLN.

Executive Mansion, *February 8, 1865.*

I think it safe to stand with Abraham Lincoln in the view he stated. This brings me to the twenty-second joint rule. The Senator from Ohio [Mr. SHERMAN] said yesterday it was adopted on the report of the Judiciary Committee. No, sir. In 1865 the House and the Senate passed, as the Senate and the House have passed this year, resolutions raising committees to ascertain and report, in the immemorial language, the mode in which the electoral votes shall be examined, and the result ascertained. Who, Mr. President, was of that committee in the House? The Senator from Ohio will remember them well when they are named. The chairman of the committee was Thaddeus Stevens, of Pennsylvania. Next on the committee was Mr. E. B. Washburne, of Illinois. Next to him was Mr. Mallory, of Kentucky. Then came Davis,—Henry Winter Davis, of Maryland; and last upon the committee was Mr. Cox. Three of these gentlemen were very pronounced republicans. In the Senate, the committee was special also, consisting of Mr. Trumbull, of Illinois, Mr. Conness, of California, and Mr. Wright, of Indiana. These two committees reported, and reported unanimously, the twenty-second joint rule. Mr. Stevens reported it in the House, and demanded the previous question upon

2 CO

it, to which nobody objected; I state this to show that no debate took place, and according to my recollection, no republican, not one, recorded himself against it. I believe no republican Senator voted against it. In the Senate the whole subject had just been elaborately debated for days on another resolution, and was well understood. Do not suppose, Mr. President, that I allude to the twenty-second joint rule to approve it. The rule is gone, and this is well; but the argument remains. The argument, like Banquo's ghost, will not down. If, by the Constitution, this province resides with the President of the Senate, the twenty-second joint rule, or any rule of the sort, and every proceeding of the Houses by which they judged of votes, has been a usurpation from the beginning as bald and wrong as unauthorized interference could be.

Under the twenty-second joint rule Senators around me heard the certificate of Arkansas read. Objection was made. Why? Because the seal impressed upon it was the governor's seal as contradistinguished from the great seal of the State; and the two Houses separated and in solemn action each House cast out the vote of Arkansas altogether, because of a supposed mistake in the seal.

Four votes from Georgia were cast out by one House alone. Why? Because, though regular in all respects, no flaw appearing on the face of the certificate, they were given for Horace Greeley, and Mr. Greeley was dead according to report.

Yes, Mr. President, these votes and others, were cast out when the result did not depend on them we are told. But is this a migratory power? Does it live in the two Houses of Congress when nothing depends upon a vote; and when everything depends upon a vote, does the power to judge that vote migrate and pass out of the two Houses and pass into the presiding officer?

I come now to another resolution. The Senator from Ohio [Mr. SHERMAN] may remember it—a resolution offered by him in January, 1873. War had ceased. The clash of arms could no longer be heard. The Supreme Court had decided that eight years before the resolution was offered, in every intent of law and fact, the war was over. Peace stood in the land; peace stood adjudged on the record. A presidential election had occurred, and on the 7th of January afterward the Senator from Ohio proposed to the Senate this resolution:

Resolved, That the Committee on Privileges and Elections is directed to inquire and report to the Senate whether the recent election of electors for President and Vice President has been conducted, in the States of Louisiana and Arkansas, in accordance with the Constitution and laws of the United States, and the laws of said States, and what contests, if any, have arisen as to who were elected as electors in either of said States, and what measures are necessary to provide for the determination of such contests, and to guard against and determine like contests in the future election of electors for President and Vice-President.

The resolution further provided in order that the answer to it may be speedy, that is to say that the information sought may be received in time to act on it in counting the electoral votes, that the committee may employ persons to take depositions, in addition to taking depositions itself. It fell to me to assign some reasons for this resolution. I wish to read briefly from what I then said as it appears in the official record. I take leave to do so, lest it may be suspected that the views I maintain are of recent growth. Here are my words in 1873:

What does it propose? To inquire whether in certain States the Constitution has, in this respect, been executed, and whether it has been executed according to its own requirements and the requirements of the laws of the United States; that is all. Keeping before us for the moment the express delegations of authority to Congress, may we not inquire whether the electors appointed are persons holding offices of trust or profit under the United States ? May we not inquire whether they were elected on the day specified? May we not inquire whether they were chosen at the place required? Undoubtedly we may. * * *

Again :

One Senator says we have a right to inquire whether the claimants are the electors appointed by Louisiana. Take it so; how are we going to find out ? Suppose it turns out that there has been no election at all ; suppose the whole election went down, trodden out under the hoof of brute violence ; suppose military power or a mob rode over the election, and there were no ballots or ballot-boxes at all, and certificates come here, may we not inquire whether those certified were in truth appointed by Louisiana?

And again :

* * * * * * *

But I go further than to maintain the naked power of Congress to inquire. I insist that we can utilize the result of the inquiry, and employ the facts in our action upon counting or refusing to count electoral votes for President and Vice-President. I see no reason to doubt that any State having provided a popular election as the mode of appointing electors, and it being alleged that no such election has been held, or that the election was a mere mockery or mob, violative not only of the laws of Louisiana, but in violation of the supreme law of the United States, we are within the scope of our power in sending a committee to find whether the allegation be fiction or fact. * * *

Once more :

To ascertain and make record of the facts, I will vote for the resolution. This alone will be wholesome ; and I will vote for it also for the use we may make of the facts in counting electoral votes, and determining any other proceeding which may come within our province.

The resolution passed, I believe without a dissenting voice. No dissent is recorded. In reply to it came a report from the Committee on Privileges and Elections. To one or two passages from that report I ask attention. It was submitted by the honorable Senator from Indiana [Mr. MORTON.] He says :

The third section of the act of Congress of 1792 declares what shall be the official evidence of the election of electors, and provides that "the executive authority of each State shall cause three lists of the names of the electors of such State to be made and certified, to be delivered to the electors on or before the first Wednesday in December, and the said electors shall annex one of the said lists to each of the lists of their votes." The certificate of the secretary of state is not required, and the certificate of the governor, as provided for in this section, seems to be the only evidence contemplated by the law of the election of electors and their right to cast the electoral vote of the State. If Congress chooses to go behind the governor's certificate, and inquire who had been chosen as electors, it is not violating any principle of the right of the States to prescribe what shall be the evidence of the election of electors, but it is simply going behind the evidence as prescribed by an act of Congress ; and, thus going behind the certificate of the governor, we find that the official returns of the election of electors, from the various parishes of Louisiana, had never been counted by anybody having authority to count them.

That, it will be observed, Mr. President, was to show that those votes could not properly be counted because the returns behind them had not been counted and certified by anybody authorized. Let me turn over and read what was said of the votes cast for the opposing electors :

The election of the Grant electors is certified by the Lynch returning board, but that board did not have the official returns before them, and their election is not certified by the governor of the State as required by the act of Congress.

Under that resolution, passed without dissent, answered by the committee, the two Houses when the day arrived proceeded to dispose of the electoral certificate of Louisiana.

Coming to a more recent period we had reported from the Committee on Privileges and Elections a bill to which reference has several times been made. I refer to it in part to call attention to the fact that only three republican members of this body voted against it, the Senator from Vermont [Mr. EDMUNDS] the Senator from Wisconsin who sits before me [Mr. Howe] and myself. What was it? A bill which would have deposited with the House of Representatives absolutely the decision of the late election, a bill which passed this body twice, which at the end of the last session was arrested only by a motion to reconsider made by a democratic Senator, but for which motion it would be necessary now only for the House to take up the bill and under the previous question pass it—the call of the yeas and nays requires forty minutes. Like Shakespeare's fairy, the House could "put a girdle round about the earth in forty minutes." Unless the President of the United States could find in the Constitution some reason for a veto, the die of this presidential election would be cast in an hour—it would have been cast e'er now.

Under the bill, the express consent of both Houses was given in advance that one House alone, without cause assigned, without examination, without anything but its *ipse dixit*, might say the vote of a State should not be counted, provided only there were conflicting certificates. There are now conflicting certificates from four States, and on these States the result depends. It has been said that this last year's bill was more guarded than the bill on our table touching the recognition it gave to conflicting certificates, or papers purporting to be certificates. I read the second section:

That if more than one return shall be received by the President of the Senate from a State, purporting to be the certificates of electoral votes given at the last preceding election for President and Vice-President in such State, all such returns shall be opened by him in the presence of the two Houses when assembled to count the votes; and that return from such State and that only shall be counted which the two Houses acting separately shall decide to be the true and valid return.

Whoever will go to the Secretary's table will find the words "and that only" introduced with the pen after the types had done their work, so as to clinch beyond peradventure the certainty that when from any State certificates, returns, or papers purporting to be certificates, conflict, no certificate shall be counted unless both Houses concur affirmatively in asserting that one certificate shall be received, and then that, and that only, shall be counted. The Senator from Indiana observed the other day that there was nothing in the bill now referred to authorizing anybody to go behind the returns, nothing authorizing anybody to go behind the electoral certificates, and that it was therefore safer than the bill before us. Mr. President, there can be but one true electoral certificate from a State unless they are duplicates. There can be but one; there cannot be two. One is genuine and one is counterfeit.

I read again from last year's bill:

And that return from such State and that only shall be counted which the two Houses acting separately shall decide to be—

What?

The true and valid return.

It is said that when Adam and Eve came from Paradise, the world was before them, and where to choose. They can have been no freer than each House would have been under that bill: unbridled, unrestricted jurisdiction is there; no metes or bounds: each House may go at large into the illimitable domain of discretion, caprice, or power. If a majority, a bare majority, of one in either House said no, that was to be the end of all consideration or controversy in respect of the vote of a State. The bill gave to one House that power which the pending bill gives to no House, that power which the committee assert for both Houses, to be exercised only when a provisional examination made by both through its trusted members, and made also by five members of the judiciary, has been fully made, and the reasons and facts given, and then retaining to the last in the two Houses the power to say whether that finding and report shall be effectual or not.

We have been told this morning that the measure before the Senate is a surrender of the rights of the republican party. I should abhor it if it were a surrender of the rights of anybody, and especially of that great party which in war and in peace has for sixteen years conducted with marvelous success the affairs of the nation. Why is it a surrender, and a surrender repugnant to those who only eight months ago were bent upon a measure which now would leave us without the ghost of a hope that the election may be declared in our favor? Why, it is a surrender because it guards the vote of every State against rejection, until both Houses, by a common tribunal, the fairest, the most learned, the most fit, the most impartial that ingenuity can invent, have investigated and found the law and the facts, and, in the light of day, with a full statement of the reasons to be spread before the world, have come to a deliberate judgment that the Constitution forbids the vote to be received. This is branded as a surrender by those who lately insisted that one House alone, in unbridled caprice, and with no statement of reasons required, might exclude a State by merely saying the vote shall not be counted. I am willing to let these two surrenders stand side by side, while the nation compares them with each other.

But, Mr. President, more recently than 1873 we have illustrations of the judgment of the two Houses of Congress touching the residence and possession of the power to ascertain and inquire into electoral votes. We have had committees sitting for weeks in the delta of the Father of Waters, and on the Atlantic coast, and a committee sitting here playing like a swivel-gun in all directions and at longer range. All this has happened during the present session. Let me read to the Senate what the Senate said in sending forth these investigating committees:

That the said committee be, and is hereby, instructed to inquire into the eligibility to office under the Constitution of the United States of any persons alleged to have been ineligible on the 7th day of November last, or to be ineligible as electors of President and Vice-President of the United States, to whom certificates of election have been or shall be issued by the executive authority of any State as such electors; and whether the appointment of electors or those claiming to be such in any of the States—

Now observe—

has been made—

The appointment of electors has been made—

declared or returned, either by force, fraud, or other means, otherwise than in conformity with the Constitution and laws of the United States, and the laws of the respective States; and whether any such appointment or action of any such elector has been in any wise unconstitutionally or unlawfully interfered with.

This language authorizes a search of the polls in voting-precincts. No inquiry can go further, and in fact the committees have been holding inquest on the registration and casting of votes, and the appliances employed to carry the elections, in several States.

For what is such inquiry? If the two Houses have nothing to do with the result, or with ascertaining whether electors were appointed, if there is nothing to be done in regard to the authenticity of the electoral certificates, if all votes the presiding officer has received, good, bad and indifferent, irrespective of quality, are to be counted, as you would count the chairs in this Chamber, why is all this?

I come now to speak of some and only of some of those who have expressed opinions on this subject, and who have expressed opinions not only authorizing the enactment of a law, but opinions irreconcilably repugnant to the idea that the presiding officer of the Senate in any contingency can lawfully exert the power in question. James Madison, Thomas Jefferson, Samuel Dexter of Massachusetts, Samuel Livermore, of New Hampshire,—he was President of the Senate; he was the colleague of John Langdon, the first President of the Senate, John Marshall, and I may add the whole Congress of 1800, Martin Van Buren, Daniel Webster, Thomas H. Benton, Stephen A. Douglas, Jacob M. Howard, Jacob Collamer, Abraham Lincoln, John J. Crittenden, Lewis Cass, Humphrey Marshall, Thaddeus Stevens, Henry Winter Davis, John Bell, and many others whose names I will not read. I will rather read the words of one whose name I did not read, but whose name, whether it be the Mill-boy of the Slashes or Harry of the West, will long kindle enthusiasm wherever in our land it is heard. I have seen in newspapers that Mr. Clay concurred in the power of the President of the Senate to determine the count of electoral votes. In 1821 Mr. Clay, as chairman of a committee, having reported a resolution which would have been absurd upon such a supposition, a resolution which stood in sharp clear denial of the power of the presiding officer, said :

The Constitution required of the two Houses to assemble and perform the highest duty that could devolve on a public body—*to ascertain who had been elected by the people to administer their national concerns.* In a case of votes coming forward which could not be counted, the Constitution was silent; but, fortunately, the end in that case carried with it the means. *The two Houses were called on to enumerate the votes for President and Vice-President; of course they were called on to decide what are votes.*

Of course says Mr. Clay, the two Houses are called upon to decide what are the votes.

It being obvious that a difficulty would arise in the joint meeting concerning the votes of Missouri, some gentlemen thinking they ought to be counted and others dissenting from that opinion, the committee thought it best to prevent all difficulty by waiving the question in the manner proposed, knowing that it could not affect the result of the election.

Again :

Mr. Clay would merely observe that the difficulty is before us ; that we must decide it when the Houses meet, or avoid it by some previous arrangement. *The committee being morally certain that the question would arise on the votes in joint meeting, thought it best to give it the go-by in this way.*

Now observe Mr. President here is the passage that has been quoted as meaning something else.

Suppose this resolution not adopted, the President of the Senate will proceed to open and count the votes; *and would the House allow that officer, simply and alone, thus virtually to decide the question of the legality of the votes ? If not, how then were they to proceed ? Was it to be settled by the decision of the two Houses conjointly or of the Houses separately ? One House would say the votes ought to be counted, the other that they ought not; and then the votes would be lost altogether.*

This is strange language for a master of statement, if he meant that the power to decide upon the validity of votes lay with the presiding officer.

Not meaning to refer by name to living men, I may schedule among the authorities all those who voted for the twenty-second joint rule in either House, all who acted under it ; especially all who voted for the bill reported by the Committee on Privileges and Elections which passed this body a few months ago, and also those who voted for the resolution under which committees are now proceeding to inquire. Did any Senator of republican faith vote against that resolution ?

Mr. President, what is the answer to this broad, deep, irresistible stream of historic precept and example ? It was given by the honorable Senator from Indiana. He said : if nothing is done, a condition of affairs will exist in which the President of the Senate, to prevent a dead-lock, must act from necessity.

The honorable Senator from Indiana has broached that doctrine before. Here it is in a report made by him on the 1st of June, 1874, a report which I infer in an unusual sense was the expression of his individual views. I observe in it these words :

So powerful have been these obligations that I believe scarce an instance is known where electors have violated these pledges.

The use of the personal pronoun there, seems to make this a personal and individual declaration, as well as a grave report from a committee. I read from it this paragraph. It cannot have been a loose opinion; chairmen of committees in the Senate do not, in writing, report loose opinions.

Clearly—

Says the author of this report—

Clearly the framers of the Constitution did not contemplate that the President of the Senate, in opening and counting the vote for President and Vice-President, should exercise any discretionary or judicial power in determining between the votes of two sets of electors, or upon the sufficiency or validity of the record of the votes of the electors in any State; but that he should perform a merely ministerial act, of which the two Houses were to be witnesses and to make record. But the exercise of these high powers may devolve upon him *ex necessitate rei.*

Supplemented by the intimation made by the Senator during this debate, we may all see what this means.

We, by refusing to make provision, are to create a necessity, and that necessity is to create a power and create a man to wield it.

The honorable Senator stigmatized the bill now before the Senate as "a contrivance." He might well have applied such a term to his own scheme of necessity. If ever there was a contrivance, if ever there was a political Hell Gate paved and honeycombed with dynamite, there it is.

Is a necessity, purposely created, to beget a power which "clearly the framers of the Constitution did not contemplate?" Is a contrived state of affairs to enthrone in this land a governing instrumentality which the Constitution does not sanction?

Is the pending bill to be defeated in order to bring on this necessity?

Mr. MORTON. Will the Senator finish the reading of the sentence? He left off reading one of my sentences.

Mr. CONKLING. I shall read the whole paragraph. The Scripture says "a contented mind is great riches," and although I know how hard it is for the Senator from Indiana to listen to a dull speech, if he will possess his soul in patience he will hear read the whole paragraph. Let me first be sure to make plain so much as I have read. The argument, but little concealed the other day, was that the pending bill should be defeated, and this would bring on a necessity, which necessity would open the way to an exercise of power, in the language of the author of this report, clearly not contemplated by the framers of the Constitution. Mr. President "necessity knows no law." Who is to decide whether he is called and chosen by necessity to be the master of an opportunity?

Necessity: that arch fiend and foe of government, that prolific mother, and apology of anarchy, revolution, despotism, and fraud, ever since human government began. The pretensions of necessity have age after age affrighted humanity, trampled on right, gendered wars, and swept realms and rulers

> Through caverns measureless to man,
> Down to a sunless sea.

Let not the representatives of American States, in this century year, connive at bringing about a necessity, they know not what, fraught with consequences they cannot order or foresee. Suppose the Speaker of the House says he is the man of destiny, that necessity has created him to untie this tangled problem. Suppose the House says it from necessity is to be the *Deus ex machina,* borrowing a phrase from the Senator from California; suppose any man or any power chooses to deem himself or itself invoked by necessity, where are the limits of such a theory? Let me read from this same report a view of some of the consequences of this so-called necessity.

There is imminent danger of revolution to the nation whenever the result of a presidential election is to be determined by the vote of a State in which the choice of electors has been irregular or is alleged to have been carried by fraud or violence, and where there is no method of having these questions examined and settled in advance—where the choice of President depends upon the election in a State which has been publicly characterized by fraud or violence, and in which one party is alleged to have triumphed and secured the certificates of election by chicanery or the fraudulent interposition of courts. *Such a President would is advance be shorn of his moral power and authority in his office, would be looked upon as a usurper, and the consequences that would result from such a state of things no man can predict.*

Mr. President, it is because I mean, at every stage which the law and the facts shall justify, to maintain that the republican nominee has been chosen Chief Magistrate of the nation; it is because I believe him to be a patriot and incapable of wishing injury or disparagement to his country, that I would have his title so clear that it can never be challenged with a pretext for believing that he, and they who supported him, meant to clutch usurped power, or dared not submit to a fair and constitutional examination the truth of the election.

Now I will read the climax of the paragraph of the report, which the Senator from Indiana wishes the Senate to hear:

But the exercise of these high powers—

The power to judge and decide between conflicting certificates, and to determine the result—

But the exercise of these high powers may devolve upon him *ex necessitate rei*, and whatever decision he may make between the two sets of electors or upon the sufficiency and validity of the record of the votes—whether on the evidence of the right of the electors to cast votes, or whether they have been cast in the manner prescribed by the Constitution—his decision is final.

And all this *ex necessitate rei*, although the framers of the Constitution meant, and meant "clearly," that he should never exert any such functions at all. This bastard child of destiny, born in the throes of an exigency specially arranged by the refusal of Congress to legislate, rising above the Constitution is to decide, and when he has decided, from the rising of the sun even to the going down of the same, there shall not be one man who does not bow mutely and reverently to his decision.

Again I say it is not for representatives of a patriotic party of law and order, in the presence of the events before which we stand, to refuse by law to constitute a peaceful, certain impartial mode under the Constitution, and above it, of ascertaining the true result of the recent election.

How shall this be done? Senators say that to ascertain the result of the election, is the attribute and duty of the two Houses. If that be the law, this bill does not overpass the law.

The pending measure has been called a compromise. If it be a compromise, a compromise of truth, of law, of right, I am against it. My life has taught me not to contrive compromises but to settle issues. Every compromise of principle, is a make-shift and a snare. It never stood; it never deserved to stand. It is the coward's expedient to adjourn to another day, a controversy easy to govern in the fountain, but hard to struggle against in the stream. If this bill be such a compromise, I am against it. But I deny that it is a compromise. I deny that it compromises anything; and, above all, that it compromises right, principle, or the Constitution. To contest a claim, is not to compromise it. To insist upon the right, and submit it to an honest, fair scrutiny and determination, is not to compromise it. A presidential election has occurred. Unless there is a tie or a failure, somebody has been chosen. To ascertain and establish the fact, is not a compromise. To reveal and establish the truth of a thing already past and fixed, is as far from a compromise as the east is from the west.

Above all, Mr. President, this is not a compromise of the position of those who hold that the two Houses as such, are bound to count the votes; and there I address a Senator who differs from me in political belief, and who opposes this bill, as do others of his faith, because he holds that the Constitution commands the two Houses to count the votes. I say the bill is no compromise by those who entertain this view. The two Houses consist of four hundred members. Four hundred men cannot each handle and scrutinize, and examine and tabulate, all the contents, true and false, of these electoral certificates. They might act by tellers. What are tellers? The eyes, the ears, the hands, the faculties of the two Houses: that is all—the proxies of the two Houses, as one may be the proxy of stockholders in a corporation. Four hundred men cannot do the mechanical or actual office of counting. They may depute two men from each House to do it; they may appoint a committee to do it. That is what our fathers proposed; they called it a grand committee. There is no harm in my saying that in committee I wished this tribunal to be called a committee: but names alter nothing. It is a committee in legal force and effect. It represents the two Houses, as tellers would represent them—no less a committee because five members of the highest judicial tribunal are part of it. Is the silver commission, at the head of which stands my distinguished friend from Nevada [Mr. JONES] less a commission of the two Houses because experts, three in number, not members of either House, belong to it? Suppose the Constitution made it the duty of Congress to observe the position of Jupiter, and a committee was appointed, of which the honorable Senator from Connecticut [Mr. EATON] ought to be one. Suppose on that committee was placed Professor Henry, to guard the Senator from Connecticut against observing Venus in place of Jupiter, [laughter,] would the committee or its character be destroyed by the presence of Professor Henry, not a member of either House? Recently a commission of the two Houses has been constituted to re-organize the Army, and on that commission are distinguished men not members of either House. Is it a void commission for that reason? If the General of the Army is on this Army commission, would any man like to go into history with it known of him that he supposed that in fact or in law the commission was impaired, or that it was not strengthened and dignified, by putting upon it the most instructed men, although they were not members of either House?

The honorable Senator from Ohio says the bill creates offices, and that the judges of the Supreme Court ought to be confirmed by the Senate. If their functions were such as he ascribed to them, I think they should at least be confirmed. He says they are "to make a President." Inasmuch as the Constitution has provided that the States and people are to do that, and has refused to allow either House to do it in the first instance, I quite concur with the Senator that they who are to make a President, ought at least to be confirmed.

Mr. SHERMAN. If I do not interrupt my friend——

Mr. CONKLING. Not at all.

Mr. SHERMAN. I will mention to him the difference between what is called the silver commission and the Army commission and this commission to make a President. When the silver commission report, their action is of no validity and either House may disregard it, and so with the report of the Army commission; but when this commission to make a President reports, it requires the affirmative action of both Houses consenting thereto to undo their work.

Mr. CONKLING. Mr. President, it often happens that when one is attempting a speech, particularly a poor speech, some Senator who interrupts him anticipates something important to another branch of the argument. When the Legislature of New York repealed the rule in Shelley's case, somebody asked Chancellor Kent why he did not strike out the chapter in his Commentaries relating to that subject? The Chancellor replied "Why, that is one of the most admired parts of the work; how could I strike it out?" And here comes the Senator from Ohio now, and is about to spoil one of the best of my points not yet reached. [Mr. SHERMAN rose.] I hope he will not do so.

Mr. SHERMAN. I will withdraw my interruption, then.

Mr. CONKLING. That is right. I hope my honorable friend will forbear, because I have a definite theory on his point. I will not take my seat without disputing his suggestion, and trying to convince a theory, fallacious it seems to me, and put forth now for the third time.

The honorable Senator from Ohio thought that these judges of the Supreme Court should be confirmed by the Senate in order to act on this commission. The Senator from New Hampshire [Mr. CRAGIN] behind me, ejaculates from his seat that "they have been once," and the remark seems to me seasonable and pertinent. They have once, on the nomination of the President and by the action of the Senate been certified; or as Mr. Benton would have said "certificated" as men selected from the whole nation for their fitness to weigh evidence, and to examine and ascertain questions of law. They are anointed with the public confidence. But the suggestion of the Senator from Ohio is that this bill establishes offices. I say that it merely appoints a commission. From time immemorial in England, from time whereof the memory of man runneth not to the contrary, parliamentary committees and commissions have been established composed not only of members, but of persons not members of either house. They are not officers in the sense intended by the Senator.

Again, was it ever heard that Congress cannot impose upon national officers additional duties? Is there any officer in the Government on whom Congress may not impose additional duties? I know the Supreme Court said, in the case of Prigg vs. The Commonwealth of Pennsylvania, that justices of the peace, being State officers, were not bound under the fugitive-slave act of 1793 to act as commissioners, but, said the court, if they choose to act it is entirely competent; not being national officers, however, Congress cannot compel them to act.

But what said the first pension law ever passed? It undertook to make the judges of the Federal courts commissioners. By a somewhat bungling phrase it spoke of "the court" and not the judges, and men queried whether under that language, denoting the court, there might not be doubt. But did anybody ever deny that Congress had power to make the judges of the Federal courts commissioners of pensions? I think it never was denied. Does the honorable Senator from Ohio doubt that Congress has power to employ a judge, whether of the court of Alabama claims, or Supreme Court, or any other court, to settle a doubtful boundary, or to exert any other faculty essential to the public welfare?

I submit to the honorable Senator from Ohio in answer to his last objection, that the two Houses, from beginning to end, make this examination. They agree beforehand to make it in a particular way, to make it by a committee. That committee incarnates the two Houses; it is in law the two Houses. By action beforehand, both Houses agree not to be finally bound by what the commission shall do; but they agree to the mode in which the examination shall be made. What is the mode? That the commission shall decide only provisionally; only conditionally. The two Houses retain the whole thing to the end absolutely in their own hands. A Senator said yesterday, and it has been repeated to-day, that if the two Houses were both required to approve by affirmative votes what the commission does, it would then be not a delegation of power—a devolution of the power of the Houses, but a retention and exercise of power by the Houses themselves.

Mr. President I deny this distinction. The power is neither more or less retained in the hands of the Houses, whether they approve the finding of the commission affirmatively, or by refusing to negative the finding. The bill provides that the examination being made by the Representatives of the two Houses, by those who constitute the eyes and ears and hands and faculties of the two Houses, and that action reported provisionally, it shall be deemed the action of the two Houses unless they disapprove it. The Supreme Court of the United States, when eight judges sit, and a decree or judgment comes up from a court below, by a foreordained rule provide that if four judges are for the decree and four against it, the decree is affirmed; it becomes the judgment of the court, nay, it virtually becomes in that case the unanimous judgment of the court. Why? Because the court, unanimously in advance, has ordered and agreed that such a division occurring, the judgment reviewed shall be affirmed. This is the rule of courts in general. A decision or finding coming before a court for reversal or affirmance, is affirmed unless a majority agree to reverse it. The honorable Senator from Indiana moves away. [Mr. CONKLING while speaking had advanced toward Mr. MORTON's desk, just across the aisle.]

Mr. MORTON. I retreated as far as I could. [Moves away.]

Mr. CONKLING. Mr. President, the honorable Senator observes that he has retreated as far as he could. That is the command laid on him by the common law. He is bound to retreat to the wall, before turning and rending an adversary; and as he has retreated as far as he could, I will repay his coyness with a reminiscence. A few months ago it was proposed in the Senate to import the Chief-Justice of the Supreme Court into the proceeding of counting electoral votes, and of him, and the presiding officers of the two bodies, to constitute a triumvirate which should be the umpire to cast the die between the two Houses when they differed about the count. The honorable Senator from Indiana voted on call of the yeas and nays for that proposition, no constitutional doubt restraining him. Does he shake his head?

Mr. MORTON. I will satisfy you on that point.

Mr. CONKLING. The Senator promises to satisfy me. He seemed to shake his head. I was about to hold up the record, to hold the mirror up to nature, and satisfy him that the chairman of the Committee on Privileges and Elections did sanction with his great weight and authority the right of the law-making power to snatch the Chief-Justice from his judgment-seat and bring him here, and make him one of a trinity which should arbitrate between the two Houses and conclude both by the vote he should give.

Returning now to the point, I repeat, Mr. President, that when a court of first instance is constituted to inquire, to hear, and report to the two Houses, and it is left with the Houses to reverse or to refuse to reverse the finding, the tribunal is provisional, and the ultimate adjudication is reserved in the two Houses; and I submit to the Senator from Ohio that, speaking in the spirit of law, it makes not the slightest difference whether the provision is that the approval of the acts of the commission shall be by affirmative action, or by withholding affirmative action. I speak in the presence of trained lawyers, and yet I speak in the presence of no lawyer who on reflection will challenge the position.

Mr. President, had I discussed, as I have not done, clearly and fully, my views in regard to this subject, I should feel better authorized to inquire how shall the two Houses exercise the power and the duty resting on them? We cannot summon the stars: we cannot command gods or angels. We must have recourse to men. We have provided that each House shall select its most trusted members. We have provided that added to these, shall be five judges of the highest court, five "sacred judges" the Senator from Ohio called them. Why "sacred?" Because they administer justice. What is the ancient and modern symbol of justice? A stony figure with blinded eyes, with an arm unmoved by a throb of feeling, holding unshaken the even scales. Because these judges are so typified, the Senator from Ohio says they are "sacred judges." Then they can be trusted. Is the proposed duty beneath them? They never sat in a greater or a graver cause. John Jay, when Chief-Justice, crossed the sea to negotiate a treaty, not so great by far as that covenant of law and peace and right which these judges are to establish. Judge Nelson sat in a commission whose duty and privilege it was to hold up before the world the attainments of America in dignity and reason, by showing that the nation was strong enough and proud enough to withdraw from the forum of brute force and passion a great question, and submit it to legally constituted authority. One of the grandest emperors on earth acted as umpire in the same proceeding, and the fifteen millions obtained by the decision, was valueless compared with the tranquillity and composure of our land for a single day—paltry indeed, by the side of the inestimable advantage of proving by actual experiment that no emergency is so great that forty-five million freemen cannot meet it calmly and safely under the free institutions they cherish. If "he who ruleth his own spirit be greater than he who taketh a city," what shall be said of the grandeur of millions who by an act as quiet as the wave of a wand can calm the commotions of a continent in an hour?

No jot or tittle of authority not reposed by the Constitution in the two Houses of Congress, acting separately or together, is broached in prescribing the jurisdiction of this commission. Familiarly in ancient and in recent times, deputing one to do an act for another, the customary phrase is "with like force and effect as if I myself did it." That in substance is the behest of this bill, with like force and effect by you who represent the two Houses for these purposes, as if the two Houses and every member were present, as the two houses of Parliament were in law present always when a full and free conference was held. The bill utters the voice of the Houses thus: To you the chosen deputies of the two Houses who on honor and on oath represent them in this investigation, we say that you are authorized to do exactly that which the two Houses, acting separately or together, themselves might do. Take the Constitution for your chart and guide. Whatever it and the now existing law commands, that do: thus far and no farther. You stand in lawyer's phrase in statu quo. Abstain from everything from which those who constituted you ought to abstain, do nothing except to deal with that which lies within the domain of constitutional duty, and report to us who repose special trust and confidence in you, all the reasons that move you, all the conclusions to which you come.

I have heard it suggested that something in this bill implies, that going behind the faculties of the States, going behind the lawful exercise of that power which the Constitution reposes in the States, and wherewith the Constitution crowns them, this commission may inquire at large, by canvassing the votes cast in parishes or even precincts, by going into the question whether those who voted were all that should have voted, whether they voted as they wished to vote—in short that the commission may become a national "returning board." The law has this ancient maxim—" that is certain which can be rendered certain." We say in this bill, "take the Constitution as it stands; that is your guide; there you will find the boundaries of your power; you shall not overpass them; execute the Constitution, and stop."

But says one Senator why does not the bill specify all the things these men are to do. To ask the question is to suggest unnumbered answers. Answers spring up as the army of Roderick Dhu sprang from the heather, when a whistle garrisoned a glen. In the first place, there is an irreconcilable difference of opinion as to the nature and extent of the power of the two Houses, or either, to pry into or penetrate the act of the States. In the next place, were all agreed, it would be impossible in a bill to embody a treatise or commentary which should provide for every contingency or possibility. It was Dean Swift who made a written schedule for his attendant of all the things he was to do; each and several his duties were set down; but on a Sunday Dean Swift fell into a ditch and called for assistance, but the attendant produced his schedule and said he found nothing there which required him to help anybody out of a ditch on Sunday. It was supposed by the committee, as the sense of its members was only finite, and very finite, that when they called, in addition to five picked men of each House, five experts in the law, men who had been selected from the great body of the nation for their training and adaptation to exploring legal distinctions and ascertaining legal truth, it was hardly worth while to attempt to accompany this trust of provisional authority with a minute bill of particulars of all the things which might be done, and how, and what in detail must not be done.

It might have been possible, by restraint and exclusion, to put fetters on these fifteen members. Every Senator who hears me knows that any attempt to run the exact boundaries of the power to admit evidence, any attempt by the concurrent action of the two Houses to agree upon a universal solvent, to come to that exact unit of accuracy in defining jurisdiction and pertinence of evidence which all would approve in advance, although a possibility in theory, would be impossible in reality.

The Senator from Massachusetts [Mr. DAWES] in a tone which few beyond me hear, inquires whether I mean that they have no limit in this bill. Mr. President I had supposed that the Constitution had raised not only a hedge and fence, but a wall of limit to the powers it confers. I supposed that when five of the most largely instructed and trusted members of the Senate, and five of the most largely instructed and trusted members of the House, were authorized to meet five judges of the highest and most largely instructed judicial tribunal of the land, we might trust to them to settle what a court of oyer and terminer settles whenever it is called upon to determine whether it has jurisdiction to try an indictment for homicide or not. I supposed that giving it the instrument by which its jurisdiction is to be measured, we could trust this provisional tribunal of selected men to run the boundary and fix the line marking their jurisdiction, and to blaze the trees. I hear a voice ask "Where they please?" This cannot have been the voice of the Senator from Massachusetts. That Senator is a lawyer, and he knows that judges cannot lawfully do anything because they please. They must stop where the law stops.

I have repeatedly insisted that the Constitution and the existing law, is the boundary; and I believe the act of 1792 is the only statute applicable. No I am wrong, the act of 1845, touching the choice of presidential electors, may also have a bearing. Inasmuch as the Constitution, the law, and the acts of Congress of which I think there are but two, prescribe the power, inasmuch as we make the existing law the guide-board, inasmuch as we command and conjure the commission to go according to the Constitution and to keep within its limits, I supposed it could not be a roving commission to traverse at large the realms of fact, superstition, and fiction.

Mr. DAWES. Mr. President, will it interrupt the Senator if I say a word?

Mr. CONKLING. Not at all.

Mr. DAWES. I hear the Senator state distinctly that this commission is to be bound by the Constitution; but I hear him state just as distinctly that in his opinion this commission, being bound by the Constitution, could not invade what I deem to be the prerogatives of the States to settle the title of their own electors. If I could hear him and all of the members of that committee make the same clear and unequivocal assertion I should be greatly comforted. My discontent and apprehension arise from the fact that while I hear him make this equally unequivocal expression of his own opinion of what the boundary is I hear others with equal distinctness and clearness and positiveness say that though they also believe this commission to be bound by the Constitution they believe the Constitution authorizes them to go into and settle questions which in my mind belong exclusively to the States to settle. That is what troubles me, and the Senator will pardon me for interrupting him in the way I have in order to get as distinctly as I could from the members of this committee, not only what I knew before every one of them would say, that the commission would have to limit the exercise of their power by the Constitution, but, inasmuch as one member of this committee believes the Constitution will stop them at one point and another member of the committee believes it will not, I suggest to the Senator would it not be safer for us by a statute to limit them? Then we shall know where the boundary is.

Mr. CONKLING. The boundary of this power is not only one of the bones of contention, but the very marrow of it. If there were no doubt in that regard, we should need no bill. If the two Houses, and the members of the two Houses, were clear and concurrent in their views, we should need no commission. It is because of an irreconcilable conflict of opinion that we propose to execute the Constitution in this way; and if I have not so said before, I want now to say that in my opinion it is not only a competent execution of the Constitution, but one substantial, effectual, and compliant with its spirit strictly. But the Senator from Massachusetts says he has heard the Senator from New York say something and the Senator from somewhere else say something; may I remind my honorable friend that what I may say in this regard, or even what he may say, is only a puff of air. The commission is to say on the oaths of its members and subject to our review what by the Constitution is committed to it. If the Senator from Massachusetts shall be of this commission, what he might think, or if I were to be of it what I might think would then be of great moment. I submit to him it is *anise* and *cumin*, and not of the weightier matters of the law, to consider what may be thought by this Senator or that Senator of the range and province within which this commission may move. They must ascertain for themselves. If the question in the State of New York is whether the court of oyer and terminer only, or also the court of sessions, has power to try indictments for homicide, no matter whether it be more or less probable that A B or C D may be convicted in one court or the other, the court passes upon the question of its jurisdiction. So this court of first instance, if it holds for example that it has no power to go behind the certificate of the governor of Oregon, that although he certified three men were electors, one of whom confessedly—I say confessedly—in the popular sense—never received a majority by which alone he could be chosen;—suppose they hold that that certificate is a barrier which neither House can pass, and that the three votes are to be counted, as certified by the governor of Oregon, so be it; and the two Houses are brought to say whether they will approve or will disapprove that decision. On the contrary suppose they say " we will go behind the certificate, we will go behind the certificate in Louisiana, not to inquire about the weight of evidence, not to find out whether the returning board found rightly or wrongly, not even to inquire whether they found honestly or corruptly, but we will go behind the certificates merely to inquire as a jurisdictional question whether the returning board of Louisiana had before it, and was authorized to act upon, the evidence of the popular will." They so report, and the honorable Senator from Massachusetts, having one vote, and a potent voice, will pass upon the report. On the contrary suppose they say they have a right to go a little further than that, and to ascertain whether the returning board of Louisiana or the governor of Oregon was moved by corrupt motive. Suppose they hold that they may search even so far, and condemn what has been done in Oregon because greed or corruption moved the hand that held the pen when the certificate was written. Upon such a ruling, the Senator from Massachusetts sitting as a member of the court of review, is to pass, on his oath and on his responsibility as a representative of a State.

Mr. DAWES. I am sincerely anxious to understand the whole scope of this bill, and if I understand the Senator aright now he states that there was in this committee an irreconcilable difference as to how far——

Mr. CONKLING. The Senator must pardon me there. I did not so state. I spoke of nothing in the committee: I spoke at large, saying that there is an irreconcilable difference of opinion. I avoided saying anything about the committee.

Mr. DAWES. I think the Senator is right. The Senator has corrected me properly. The Senator says the committee recognized an irreconcilable difference upon how far the Constitution will permit this commission to go into an investigation of matters that belong to the States. To meet that irreconcilable difference, as I understand him to say, they propose in the bill to take the construction of the Constitution from this commission.

Mr. CONKLING. Mr. President, the Senator from Massachusetts is too astute not to know, too alert to forget, that he who in advance can exactly fix and measure the limits and application of constitutional authority, holds in his hands the horoscope in which may be read with some distinctness the final issue of the whole matter. It was the purpose and the laborious effort of the committee, to establish a provisional tribunal, from which should come, with impartiality as great as could be obtained by the instrumentalities of humanity, a result conforming to law and to the facts, a result resting neither on the wishes of the Senator from Massachusetts nor on the wishes of the most pronounced opposing partisan, but resting on the Constitution and the law as they were on that day in December—I believe it was the 6th,—when the electors in all the States cast their votes. The sole object was to devise an instrumentality to reveal and establish, historically and constitutionally, the truth and fact of a past transaction. For us to undertake in advance to say definitely and in detail, what this commission should decide, was to abandon the attempt to present a measure which would command the approval of the fourteen members of the two select committees, and afterward of the Senate and the House with their four hundred members, and at last of that great constituency which stands behind us all. We held that a tribunal fit to be intrusted even provisionally with passing upon any part of this controversy, was fit to be intrusted with judging of their own powers after we had delivered into their hands, as their chart and compass, the Constitution and law of the United States, and told them to stand to and abide by that in every contingency.

If the honorable Senator from Massachusetts proposes to launch on the heady currents of debate in these Houses, the question what at every step would be correct in the proceedings of the commission, I say to him he proposes to set sail on a soundless and shoreless sea; the 4th of March, 1877, the 4th of March, 1878, would not see the end of a debate attempting to predict the solution of inquiries so intricate, varied, and entangled. We left the commission, as the law of Massachusetts leaves to the lowest court which in the first instance tries a man on a charge involving his life or his liberty, to determine whether it has power to entertain indictments for offenses such as that. We left it as the law leaves the most menial civil tribunal to determine whether, and how far it has power to entertain a controversy, the most insignificant, arising between one man and another, whether one owes the other money or not. The Senator in a subdued voice now suggests the accuracy with which the jurisdiction of courts is asserted in the State of Massachusetts and he bids me make this as accurate as things are made in the State of Massachusetts. Mr. President, the sentiment of despair is the only sentiment produced by such an appeal. The idea of the representatives of all the States making anything as exact as things are made in the State of Massachusetts! [Laughter.] The Senator says that I stated we have done as is done in Massachusetts. I did not mean that. It was the Queen of Sheba who said that she never realized the glory of Solomon until she entered the inner temple. The idea that the representatives of other States could breathe its upper air, or tread the milky-way, never entered into the wildest and most presumptuous flight of imagination. O no, Mr. President. Whenever the thirty-seven other States attain to the stature of the grand and old Commonwealth, the time will come when no problem remains to be solved, and when even contested presidential votes will count themselves. [Laughter.] Then in every sphere and orbit everything will move harmoniously, by undeviating and automatic process.

Mr. President, I owe an apology to the Senate, and I make it feelingly, for the time occupied in this discussion.

I signed this report. I will vote for the pending bill; vote for it, denying that it is a compromise, believing that it is no compromise, believing that it surrenders the rights of none, and maintains the rights of all. It seems to me fair and just. Adopted, it composes the country in an hour. The mists which have gathered in our land will be quickly dispelled; business will no longer falter before uncertainty or apprehension. If thoughts of anarchy or disorder, or a disputed chief magistracy, have taken root, the passage of the bill will eradicate them at once. The measure will be a herald of order and calmness, from sea to sea; it will once again proclaim to the world that America is great enough, and wise enough, to do all things decently and in order. It may be denounced by partisans on the one side and on the other; it may be derided by the adventurous and the thoughtless; it may be treated with courageous gaiety, as it has been by the honorable Senator from Pennsylvania; it may not be presently approved by all the thoughtful and the patriotic. Still I will vote for it, because I believe it executes the Constitution, and because I believe it for the lasting advantage of all the people and of all the States, including that great State whose interests and whose honor are so dear to me. It may be condemned now, but time at whose great altar all passion, and error, and prejudice at last must bow, will test it, and I believe will vindicate it. Those who vote for it can wait. Yes, they can wait.

Senators: in a matter of duty so exalted, we may "place our bark on the highest promontory of the beach, and wait for the rising of the tide to make it float."

www.ingramcontent.com/pod-product-compliance
Lightning Source LLC
Chambersburg PA
CBHW032122080426
42733CB00008B/1019